106

THE CHRISTIAN NEW MORALITY

The Christian New Morality

Morality

A Biblical Study of Situation Ethics

O. SYDNEY BARR

New York
OXFORD UNIVERSITY PRESS
1969

Copyright © 1969 by Oxford University Press, Inc.
Library of Congress Catalogue Card Number: 69-17758
Printed in the United States of America

To
Margaret, Joyce, and Mark

Preface

This is a book about the New Morality or, as it is alternatively called, Situation Ethics. It springs from my conviction that this contemporary and controversial phenomenon is at its root deeply Christian, and furthermore that it offers a principle for ethical decision-making which is of the highest significance for the kind of world in which we live today. In particular, these pages are addressed to the New Morality's fundamental affirmation: Love must be the starting point and dominant control for every facet of human existence.

But the word "love" requires careful and rigorous defining. Actually, of course, as used by Situation Ethics, it refers to Christian love. And for this, as informed advocates of the New Morality frequently point out, our chief source of information is the New Testament and especially its picture of Jesus the Christ. The New Morality, for that matter, insists that Holy Scripture itself demands love's absolute priority. Needed, however, is an easily available study that examines this claim in depth and systematically sets forth those New Testament criteria that determine what Christian love is and does.

To this end, in the first chapter I have described as simply

as possible the basic affirmations of the New Morality, at the
same time endeavoring to pierce the most common misappre-
hensions that this phrase conjures up in the minds of so many.
In Chapters II, III, and IV the role and the nature of love, as
exemplified by the life and ministry of Jesus, are discussed in
detail, first as they are seen in the Gospels According to Matthew, Mark, and Luke, then in the teaching and missionary
activity of St. Paul, and finally in the Gospel According to John
and the three Johannine Epistles. Chapter V underlines and
illustrates my own persuasion that the Christian New Morality, far from being a temporary fad, is an ethical stance that
merits earnest consideration. One need not agree with all its
proposals to recognize that its focusing upon biblical love
underlines and communicates the heartbeat and the urgency of
the age-old gospel. Consequently, it demands and makes possible far-reaching Christian renewal. Moreover, the flexibility
with respect to past experience and past tradition, which one
finds to be indigenous to that love that is depicted in the New
Testament, holds out special promise for an age such as ours,
an age which is markedly open-ended and therefore begs for
open-mindedness on the part of us all. I suggest that the
Christian New Morality has dimensions and creative possibilities that far exceed what is generally recognized even by its
staunchest supporters.

The reader, then, will find in these pages none of the sensationalism that characterizes so many treatments of this subject. I have cited no case histories—except those so plentifully
supplied by the New Testament itself. Technical pros and
cons, and the controversies that swirl around Situation Ethics
generally have been deliberately put aside. None of these really
matters, nor is future discussion about the New Morality with
all of its many ramifications likely to continue fruitful, unless
and until we clarify that underlying premise upon which all
else rests—the claim that the New Testament itself affirms that
love is the only inviolable "law," and the sole ultimate criterion

for man's every thought, word, and deed. Can this claim be substantiated? The question is a crucial one, and I hope that the
present investigation will encourage other students of Holy
Scripture to examine the biblical record with the same query
in mind.

There will, of course, be those who say that an ethic based
solely upon love is too vague and too idealistic. And it has
been charged, with some justification, that advocates of this
position have frequently been too "simplistic" in their approach to ethical problems. But it is important to note that
there is nothing in the following pages that denies the desir-
ability or the practical necessity of laws, secular as well as religious, which will serve as invaluable guidelines for human
conduct and activity. Adherents of Situation Ethics themselves
(although not as loudly as one might wish) affirm such a need
as imperative, and quite rightly, in this connection, point to
the New Testament and its record of Jesus' own positive evaluation of the laws of his day. Many will also demur that the
day by day application of total loving concern for others is
awesomely difficult. And so it is; after all, the chief biblical
symbol of love is Good Friday's cross. But the Christian will,
on the other hand, gratefully recall that the same gospel which
demands total love for others also proclaims the good news of
God's enabling grace. This, too, is the message of the cross.
And it points to a dimension of the Christian ethical experience that the New Morality might well consider more fully
than in the past.

Finally, in the hope of reaching as broad a spectrum of
readers as possible, I have sacrificed the elaborate argumenta-
tion which in a more technical study would naturally be expected in connection with the interpretation of some of the
biblical texts cited. It seemed unwise in a book of this nature
to burden its pages with such complexities. By no means, of
course, is the gospel picture of Jesus an exact replica of what
we would have seen or heard had we been there at the time.

Rather, the Evangelists depict for us the way in which the early church remembered Jesus, thereby bequeathing to us many uncertainties about what Jesus actually said and did, and about how we are to understand the record as we read it today. And yet I am utterly convinced that beneath it all we can see clear lines of the person that Jesus was and—the crux of the matter for our purposes—can affirm beyond all doubt that total love for God and for all of mankind was the dynamic center around which his own human life revolved. Doubtless many of the "Jesus sayings" which I have quoted and commented upon in this book did not come verbatim from his lips; and yet one can confidently presume what I like to call their "essential authenticity" because they are so demonstrably in accord with such minimal knowledge about the Jesus who lies in the background as is available to us. Increasingly today we are recognizing that a literalistic and mechanical proof-text use of Holy Scripture is impossible. Still, however, the Bible speaks to our own time and circumstances as, hopefully, the following pages will suggest.

I am happy to have the opportunity to acknowledge the help and kindness of so many who, without perhaps realizing it, have contributed to this book. These include colleagues as well as students who in informal discussion and in the classroom have challenged me at many points and at the same time have encouraged me to continue. Those who read this manuscript in its earlier stages, if they consent to read it anew, will recognize how indebted I am to their interest and to their counsel.

New York   O. S. B.
February 1969

Contents

I

Love and the New Morality

What is the New Morality?

We read about it in newspapers and popular magazines. Conferences are organized around it. Strong sermons discuss it pro and con. Its mention immediately brings to mind the Kinsey Report, *Playboy* magazine, and the sexual revolution. In its name, it seems, anything and everything manages to find justification. On the other hand, a greater number of people simply shrug it off with the glib conclusion, "The New Morality is simply the old immorality in a new garb."

Such easy dismissal, however, is a mistake. There is no flippancy on the part of those who are its serious advocates. Many of them are highly intelligent and committed Christians. Their position is one that has been carefully considered, and it represents a significant landmark in the history of ethics. Furthermore, the New Morality's question-asking stance concerning the accepted norms of human conduct is part of that over-all ferment which today is challenging every traditional expression of Christian faith and life. It is animated, at least in part, by the exaggerated flux of the times in

knowledge and circumstances that
begging problems never before en-
. Christian ethic, and by the convic-
ave been right and good for the past
stly inadequate for a fast-changing
lity as a popular fad will disappear.
onalism there lies a new and force-
rspective about which we shall hear
n the years immediately ahead. The
come more apparent as, hopefully, in
the following pages ... succeed in piercing the exaggeration
and emotionalism which surround this controversial matter
and come to understand its underlying rationale and genuine
human concern. Agree or disagree, it is important that we
understand its challenge.

The phrase New Morality is a popular and badly misunderstood designation for what is better described as the Situation
Ethic. Its basic premises are as follows:

1. *Persons are more important than things.* The potential
that we have to become and remain "persons" who are free,
responsible, and to a considerable degree in control of ourselves
and our environment is a precious gift of God, and one of
those fundamentals that distinguishes man from the rest of
creation. Laws, on the other hand, are "things," obviously
important because they are essential to the structuring of
community, and yet possessing the capability of destroying
that which is more important than any law—people. When,
therefore, a law conflicts with the God-given right to be a full
person, it must give way, no matter how tried and true and
sacred it may be.

2. *Love alone is the ultimate criterion for making ethical
decisions.* It is this statement, above all others, which makes it
so difficult for the New Morality to obtain a fair hearing. More
often than not it is assumed that "love" here means affection,

and therefore that this is an ethic concerned chiefly, and dubiously, with promoting permissiveness regarding sexual habits. Such, however, is most emphatically not the case. The love affirmed by the Situation Ethic as the one "law" that must never be broken is the direct opposite of desire and getting for one's self. It is, rather, a self-giving out of total concern in action for the best good of another. All other criteria for human activity that have been codified into laws, either sacred or profane, are relative. In other words, their value is not inherent, but will wax and wane according to time and circumstance. Again, when law and love contradict each other, one must choose the course dictated by love.

3. *What love demands in any specific instance depends upon the situation.* From this premise comes the less misleading descriptive phrase for the New Morality, namely, the Situation Ethic. Thus, adherents of the New Morality are properly called "situationists." This is to say that the context of an action is highly significant; concern for others' best good will not always dictate the same solution to the same problem. What is the most loving thing for one generation or culture or member of a family may not be so for a different generation or culture, or even a second member of that same family. This assertion is especially pertinent today. During the past fifty years or so the over-all world situation, because of the sudden burgeoning of new techniques, new science, and new communications, has changed beyond all imagination. Is what was good in the past still the best good for the present? Will it remain so for tomorrow? For situationists these are key questions.

4. *The New Morality is biblical morality. Behind it lies the authority of Jesus Christ himself.* Actually, the claim is made, to insist that love is the sole ultimate determiner of all human activity is, and always has been, the only truly Christian basis for any ethical system. This, of course, is to affirm that the New Morality at heart is actually not new at all. It is with

this claim in particular that the following chapters are
concerned.

These four premises will readily suggest that the New Morality has a significance far greater than can be recognized by
those who equate it simply with matters of sexual conduct.
This is not to suggest that sex is outside its province. Inevitably, since his chief concern is persons and sexuality is integral
to personhood, the situationist's refusal to idolize past customs
and patterns of behavior that have become sacrosanct through
long use, leads him to look searchingly at traditional sexual
mores and practices. Thus, situationists, employing the criterion of effectual concern for the best good of persons, have
generally been vigorous supporters of efforts to reform laws
having to do with divorce, birth control, abortion, homosexu-
ality, and such like. But the same criterion is directly relevant
to a host of other problems which contemporary changes have
brought to the fore, problems that quite literally hold the key
to the continued existence of individuals as persons rather
than as "things" in a truly free yet responsible society.

Today, for example, anyone truly concerned about personhood cannot but ask important questions of our traditional
view of man and his labor. Aware that automation and cyber-
netics are rapidly invading almost every corner of life, and
faced with the imminent prospect that leisure will become the
principal occupation of most individuals, can we continue to
make the sacred equation "income=work=virtue"? And what
does this suggest concerning our aims and methods for education? If man himself is not to become a meaningless autom-
aton, we must squarely face the responsibility of enabling
people who no longer work for their living to exist, nevertheless, fully and creatively as persons. Or, to take another
example, we possess today far greater awareness than we had
in previous generations about what constitutes a person and
his well-being. Does this perhaps suggest that we need care-

fully to rethink the wide range of traditional sexual taboos? Or, from a different perspective, if we genuinely wish our young people to act responsibly in sexual matters, what does concern for their best good suggest about the current "ethic" that condones heavy reliance in the field of advertising upon sexual stimulation to make the cash registers ring? Is a judicial system that is still largely punitive (under the guise of protecting the community) the sum total of our obligation to transgressors of the law who are no less persons than ourselves? We now possess psychological, sociological, and medical knowledge and techniques which make abortion, birth control, and artificial insemination practical and safe everyday possibilities. Does not all this add new dimensions to our ability and obligation to effect great good for thousands of people who, until recently, were forced by ignorance to live in fear, want, and frustration? Is it "loving" to permit the advertising, or even the manufacture, of products that have been proved harmful to mental or physical well-being? We now have nuclear power. Can it ever again be said that there is such a thing as a morally defensible war?

Here, then, are current problems, all of which are critical because they involve not just material well-being, but the essential personhood of millions upon millions both present and future. In some of these areas progress has already been made; and often, it should be underlined, recognition that persons are ultimately far more important than even the most sacred customs and precepts of the past has been the motivating force. This again indicates that the New Morality is indeed not that "new" after all. Because these and many other such matters that are intimately related to human well-being concern the very fabric of our culture, it is plain that the Situation Ethic cannot be dismissed in a cavalier fashion. On the contrary, it has appeared in our midst not as a weak concession to the confusion of the times in which we live, but rather as a positive attempt to supply a criterion of motivation and decision. Many believe that the New Morality's insistence upon the absolute priority of love is precisely the breakthrough that we badly need in order to deal creatively with a future so uncertain and yet so full of alternative possibilities for good or evil.

In the light of this potential, it is indeed unfortunate that the New Morality is so frequently dismissed out of hand. But it is not difficult to discover why this happens. Many, as we have already suggested, equate the New Morality principally with the relaxation (desirable or irresponsible, according to one's viewpoint) of sexual mores. This misunderstanding is abetted to no small extent by the use, perhaps unavoidable, of a vocabulary which is widely misinterpreted. Also, the fact that situationism raises pointed questions about certain precepts which Christians have traditionally held to be divinely revealed for all time frequently causes an emotional rather than a reasoned response to its challenge. Furthermore, the four premises that we noted at first glance beg certain disturbing questions: Is not the Situation Ethic wholly arbitrary? Does it not make human activity depend solely upon the unstable whim and fancy of the moment? Does not the situationist invite moral and social anarchy? How can one possibly say that the Bible, which gives us the Ten Commandments and numerous other forceful "thou shalts" and "thou shalt nots," authoritatively supports the affirmation that love is the only injunction which must never be broken? As a first step toward answering such queries, we must look briefly at the principal misconceptions which cause so many to berate the New Morality without ever really determining what it is all about.

1. The very word "morality" is a stumbling block. To the man on the street this term has, predominantly, a sexual connotation. A "morals charge," for example, involves sexual

offences. As a result of this popular usage, many people initially and automatically make the mental equation "New Morality=New Sex," usually with the implication that the whole business is just too naughty for words. This misconception is aggravated by another factor: Sex is such an intimate and, therefore, emotional concern, that objective thinking in this area is especially difficult to achieve. Nor does it help matters that public communications media when discussing the New Morality employ, for obvious reasons, a preponderance of examples draw from the problems which man has with his sexuality.

It is important, therefore, to remember that by dictionary definition morality is a summary word which speaks of *every* area of human conduct and relationships. Such is its intended use by the New Morality. We have already had occasion to see that situationism challenges man's thinking and previous patterns of action in the fields of jurisprudence or international relations no less than in the area of family affairs. It speaks to the technical revolution no less than to the sexual revolution. It is an undeniable fact of history that as the years pass by what was at one time workable or profitable must often be discarded. So today, the situationist holds, we are fenced in by many customs and prejudices of a former time which are simply no longer viable, and which often subject individuals and entire ethnic groups to hardship and indignity. New knowledge and new awareness suggest the possibility of changes in methods and goals. And, the Situation Ethic insists, the criterion of love demands such changes.

2. This word "love," however, also poses serious difficulties. So thoroughly have Hollywood, Madison Avenue, and popular journalism shaped our thinking that the mere mention of love for a vast majority conjures up a never-never land of sentimentality and romance. Again, the facile equation made by so many between the New Morality and sexual gratification

is hardly surprising. And in such a climate of opinion situationism's convenient summary slogan, "nothing matters but love," is widely misunderstood.

It cannot be emphasized too strongly, therefore, that the love which is central to the Christian New Morality has as its measure the kind of love that we find in the New Testament. The technical term often used—it is simply a transliteration of the Greek word most frequently employed in the biblical text—is *Agape*. And such love—Christian love—has a breadth and a depth incomprehensible to soap box scenarios. As we shall see at length in succeeding chapters, it is compounded of many things. Its root, however, is not feeling, self-gain, or self-gratification, but the will which impels one to action in behalf of others. Its model (and source of strength) is Jesus Christ himself.

This is not, one hastens to add, all that can or should be said. Openness to receive and the joy of receiving are as much necessities for fullness of living as is the ability to give, and equally an integral part of the biblical concept of love in its totality. For that matter, the best example in human experience of this fundamental principle of existence is sexual love, which maturely and responsibly shared is not only great joy but man's richest intimation of that divine love to which Christian faith points as the very essence of God himself. Nevertheless, an indispensable beginning to such mutuality, and essential to its growth to maturity, is the earnest giving of one's self with stubborn persistence in response to another's need even when there is no expectation of a return or of personal gain. It is this particular aspect of Christian love which is the Situation Ethic's primary concern. *Agape*, then, is manifestly relevant and applicable to every area of human involvement. To equate the New Morality merely with sex or, even worse, with the encouraging of sexual laxity, is a sad misreading of the facts.

3. Some are convinced that the Situation Ethic's refusal to

absolutize any law, no matter how long-standing or sacred, and its insistence that *Agape* may demand, in particular situations, that one break the law, are nothing more than a thinly disguised subjective rationalization for doing whatever one's fancy of the moment suggests. By way of rebuttal, situationism affirms that its anti-legalism is a freedom-with-responsibility, and claims, as we shall see, to be grounded in that freedom-for-service which is so strongly emphasized by St. Paul. Even more striking is that it is to the Christ who lived and died as the servant of all that the Christian situationist looks when he seeks to determine what love, freed from subservience to legalism, is and demands and does. Not anything that pleases, but what Christ pleases—this is the criterion of the New Morality.

4. Many fear that the Situation Ethic's relativism is an invitation to civil, social, and moral anarchy. If, as is theoretically possible, solutions to a given problem will vary widely because of the almost infinite diversity of circumstances in which love must be applied, it would seem that any possibility of social structure and ordered community is seriously threatened.

The rejoinder here is the sensible reminder that, before one can know in any given instance what is the best good for all concerned, he must first answer the question, "What *is* the situation?" To this end it is necessary to ascertain as much as possible about all of the contingencies. Not only does this require knowledge regarding the persons involved, but it also necessitates awareness concerning possible consequences for the foreseeable future as well as for an immediate present. Furthermore, no situation involving individuals can be divorced from the ever-present context of community. Every decision must reckon with the inescapable fact that what is for a given person's best good is indissolubly linked with the best good of the society of which he is a part. To find out what love demands, then, is no easy assignment. The circumstances which lead to and surround decision-making are often extremely complex, especially today. The necessity for cognitive effort—the principle of love applied with reason—is almost overwhelming in its demand. Clearly this is not a context in which arbitrariness can flourish, nor is such strenuous reasoned concern as this the kind of climate that breeds social and moral anarchy.

5. Lastly, and closely related, is the surprising assumption of not a few that the Situation Ethic has no use for laws or codes. Anyone who has read in context what the proponents of the New Morality have to say knows that such is not the case. True, the situationist affirms that no law is inviolable, nor is there any problem for which the correct solution is invariably the same. To treat past or present lists of "do's" and "don'ts" as completely inflexible is to make them ends in themselves, and is an idolatry which does irreparable harm to persons, physically, mentally, and spiritually. To assume, moreover, that the codes which strive to preserve the best good for one generation will automatically serve the same end for the next is to run the risk of foreclosing the future by inhibiting that openness which is so essential for creative adaptation to new circumstances. Nevertheless, it is a matter of record that situationists repeatedly stress the value of past experience and precedents in matters of conduct. They recognize also that legislation is essential to the ordered structure of any society, and that to have guidelines which serve as aids in the decision-making process is an imperative necessity in the human situation.

The New Morality, that is, pleads not for the elimination of laws, but for flexibility in their application. It calls, as well, for that kind of openness which is able to recognize the need for change, and therefore will not hesitate, when new situations dictate, to replace old laws with new legislation which will channel concern for others' best good more effectively. Always, however, there is this important caveat: Never must we allow ourselves to absolutize such useful norms. Laws as such, whether they be old or new, possess no inherent quality of goodness or badness. Their one purpose is to make possible and to accomplish that which love for persons demands. The needs of people change, and so do circumstances and situations. That which is for an individual's best good also changes. Therefore, what love requires, ultimately, depends upon the situation. And yet, as guidelines for the immediate present, codes are of the highest significance, and no true situationist has ever held otherwise.

When one avoids such common pitfalls as those just noted, it is possible to examine the New Morality more objectively. Clearly, we are concerned here with something which goes far deeper than its sensational popularized image suggests. It is also apparent that the basic position which it advocates is not an extremist one. To be sure, the implications are far-reaching; situationism's overriding concern for persons asks pointed questions about many inherited patterns of activity which for most of us are second nature. Nevertheless, the Situation Ethic takes a position midway between two opposite poles.

To its left, for example, stands antinomianism. This is the view that man is bound by no law whatsoever. "I am free," the antinomian shouts, "I can do as I please!" This view fails to recognize an obvious fact of life—that freedom for one's self, unless exercised responsibly with regard for the like freedom of others, is totally illusory. The antinomian's "freedom" is subjective and completely selfish. In every situation he says, "Me first," with the inevitable result that he manipulates others, viewing them not as persons and ends in their own right, but as mere means for his own gratification.

The Christian situationist on the contrary says, "I am free —to serve others." Unlike the antinomian, he relies heavily upon past experience and present norms—but always flexibly; because he refuses to submit himself or others to that dehumanization which inevitably results when laws are allowed to become the gods of one's existence. His anti-legalism, however, is a responsible one because he has an allegiance to something other than himself—*Agape*. Thus, his vocation is not to self-indulgence, but to unfettered insistence upon that good which will most effectively enable others to become and remain their full selves.

On the situationist's right hand stands the legalist. It is his conviction that there are certain fundamental laws ingrained in the universe (natural law) or revealed in Holy Scripture (the Ten Commandments, for example) which are immutable for all time and for all peoples, and never, under any circumstances, to be disobeyed. Theoretically, the legalist says, when law and love appear to be irreconcilable, it is the former which must be satisfied, and in the final analysis actions are right or wrong not because they are "loving" or "unloving," but because they conform or do not conform to the code. Legalists, one hastens to add, may well seek in every way possible to apply the law with kindness and mercy. Not infrequently do we find its adherents themselves advocating the way of love in preference to exacting the technicality of the law. Such action, however, is viewed negatively as being the lesser of two evils; whereas the situationist regards such considered opting for love as a positive good. A strict legalism insists that in the long run, no matter what the immediate effects in terms of personal hardship or degradation, the best good for all concerned in particular problem situations lies in compliance with those pre-determined solutions which the law sets forth.

The situationist's answer takes many forms. Of first importance is the claim, examined in the following chapters, that Holy Scripture itself makes the letter of the law subservient to the demands of *Agape*. Apart from this, many would object that the phrase "in the long run," which we employed just above, reflects a hidden and highly dubious premise: The only truly important thing for man is that hoped-for future which lies beyond the grave. Without in any way denying the significance of the traditional hope, it is important to remember that the total Christian gospel speaks with equal persuasion and meaning to man's "here and now," to people's *present* joys, sorrows, hardships, needs, and well-being. The words cited by St. John, "I came that they may have life, and have it abundantly," refer to man's earthly life, and represent a conviction that is expressed throughout the New Testament (Jn. 10:10). A hard and fast legalism, however, by insisting upon unqualified adherence to the letter of the law, often suppresses legitimate hope for the present. It is unbiblical because it denigrates life and inhibits that potential for responsible and full existence in this world which has been given to man by God himself. Laws are indeed necessary; but when, as happens in an imperfect society, they prevent rather than abet the responsible exercise of love, they must give way.

The situationist, moreover, cannot but wonder whether the legalist recognizes the radical nature of what is going on around him, and whether, even, he is fully aware of the changes which are upturning every corner of the globe. There are some who look upon today's challenges to the traditional Christian ethic with suspicion, often and vaguely attributing such questioning to modern man's supposed deterioration. Frequently their answer is to rush to the defence of "the faith" and to reinforce all of the traditional rules. Others, by way of reply, insist that such a morbid view of man's present state is unjustified. No Christian will deny that there is sin in the world. It is far more realistic, however, to recognize that current dissatisfaction with the status quo is the inevitable and salutary result of changes on the contemporary scene which are far more revolutionary and widespread than one could possibly have anticipated even a generation ago. It is undeniable that what served the best good of people in years past in many instances inhibits meaningful life today. The circumstances under and through which man can be that full self which God wills are, in our time, vastly different from what they were fifty years ago.

Both antinomianism and legalism, but especially the latter, have played significant roles throughout Christian history beginning with the New Testament church itself. It is noteworthy, too, that Christian moralists, generally, down through the ages have been troubled by legalism's rigidity. As a direct result of this we have the phenomenon known as casuistry. According to Webster's *New Collegiate Dictionary,* casuistry is a technical term meaning the "science or doctrine of dealing with cases of conscience and of resolving questions of right or wrong in conduct." A second definition reflects the more usual pejorative use of the word: "sophistical, equivocal, or specious reasoning, especially in regard to law or morals." This latter definition reminds us of something that has characterized Christian moral theology for centuries, namely, the employment of highly ingenious methods to get around the law while still technically respecting its inviolability. A typical example, and one still in vogue, is the practice of allowing the re-marriage of one or both parties to a divorce by declaring that for certain specific reasons their previous marriage was in fact no marriage, thereby technically preserving the sacred precept that wedlock is irrevocably a lifelong union.

Although its deviousness is often derided, and sometimes with good reason, what casuistry testifies to is of genuine significance. At its best, it is an attempt to respond to that good sense informed by sensitivity and experience which has always made deep-thinking Christians restless with an unimaginative legalism. Our previous example is a case in point: Casuistry protects the law, and yet seeks as far as possible to mitigate its hardness out of a consideration for people as persons. Thus, it witnesses to the recognition, however inchoate, that *Agape* rather than law must dominate human relationships and that *Agape* is ultimately the only criterion for ethical decision-making. Again, it is apparent that advocates of the New Morality are not the first to insist upon the priority of love.

love is the primitive - for the New morality!

There is, however, another reason for suggesting that the New Morality is not so new after all. As we noted in the fourth premise the Situation Ethic points to Holy Scripture, and particularly to its record of the life and teaching of Jesus, as the ultimate justification of its position. This, if verifiable, immediately indicates that the phrase New Morality is something of a misnomer. It may well be, as today's situationists aver, that a thoroughgoing application of *Agape* would demand significant modification of many current policies and practices; and the result could properly be termed "new." At the same time, Christian situationism's heavy reliance upon the Bible means that at least by intent it is leading the way to the recovery of an important aspect of the gospel that has been neglected or forgotten.

The New Morality's biblical orientation has a further significance. When the Christian situationist says that changing times leave us no choice but the intelligent and prayerful application of the basic principle "nothing matters but love," he is not being a defeatist or sounding a frustrated signal for retreat before the confusions of the later twentieth century. On the contrary, he is reading the signs of the times boldly and confidently and in the context of a deep Christian faith. He is proclaiming that the baffling complexities of life today are a work of the Holy Spirit challenging men to a new recognition of the basic Christian gospel as manifested in Jesus Christ: God is love, God loves his universe, and love, which St. Paul recognizes as the chief manifestation and activity of the Spirit, is *the* principle and power which creates all things, sustains all things, gives meaning to all things, and opens men's hearts to that present and future which, no less than the past, are the Lord's.

When all is said and done, however, the question remains: Is the New Morality correct in affirming biblical and dominical authority for its position? In the pages that follow our primary purpose is to explore significant portions of the New

Testament in an attempt to determine if this claim can be substantiated. The question, of course, is absolutely key, and is of the greatest possible consequence. Upon its answer will depend our judgment as to whether or not the New Morality is indeed "Christian" and therefore, despite the pain which it may cause to old traditions and to old prejudices, to be welcomed and put to work.

II

Jesus: Law or Love?

It is self-evident that any ethic claiming the name "Christian" must be grounded in the teaching and activity of Jesus himself. As our first task, therefore, we must examine the church's memory of his life and ministry as recorded in the gospels. That he spoke of God's love, enjoined love upon his hearers, and was himself deeply concerned for others are facts familiar to all who have read the New Testament. The New Morality's basic premise, however, will not let us stop here. It maintains that love is so fundamental that it must take precedence over every other "good," no matter how imperative, known to human experience. What would Jesus have said about this? Was he a situationist? What demand did love make upon his own life? and why? These are the questions immediately before us, and they require that we scrutinize the biblical sources with as much care and objectivity as possible.

One of the primary causes for rejoicing on the part of early Christians was the new freedom which Christ had brought. St. Paul wrote, "For freedom Christ has set us free" (Gal. 5:1).

And these words are typical of both the stunning awareness of release from the past and the sense of a completely fresh beginning which characterized the Christian's vision of his new life. The New Testament, however, also shows that there were Christians who failed to understand what this freedom involved and misused it. There is clear evidence that not a few adopted precisely that antinomian view which we noted in the previous chapter. That is, freedom from the past was interpreted as freedom from responsibility. Consequently, the writers of the New Testament found it necessary to exhort their readers to a proper acceptance of the ethical obligation which was an integral part of the Christian life.

This erroneous equation of freedom with self-indulgent license may come as a surprise. A first glance at the gospels, at any rate, shows that the pattern of Jesus' own life and teaching categorically denies any such attitude. For there is nothing more characteristic of Jesus than his sense of responsibility and obedience to something other than himself, his personal living of the injunction, "You shall worship the Lord your God, and him only shall you serve" (Mt. 4:10; Lk. 4:8). His mission, he knew, was not of his own conceiving; it was God who had commissioned him: "Thou art my beloved Son; with thee I am well pleased" (Mk. 1:11; Lk. 3:22). He sought nothing for himself, but only to share with others the good news about God: God's reign is "for real," its power of forgiveness and restoration does in truth penetrate the world of man's affairs and frustrations and yearnings. "My teaching is not mine, but his who sent me"; "Truly, truly, I say to you, the Son can do nothing of his own accord, but only what he sees the Father doing; for whatever he does, that the Son does likewise"—these words show how completely foreign antinomian license ("I am free to do as I please") was to Jesus' thinking and manner of living (Jn. 7:16; 5:19). From the time of his baptism in the Jordan River and temptation in the wilderness until the agony in Gethsemane and on the cross one aim was dominant: "not my will, but thine, be done" (Lk. 22:42).

Equally "un-antinomian" was Jesus' high regard for the religion which he inherited from his forbears, and his acknowledgment of its claim upon himself. He firmly believed that the sacred writings of the Old Testament were divinely inspired and contained the revealed will of God, and he quoted from them frequently. His own teaching and understanding of his task were expressed in the familiar terms of contemporary Judaism. He worshipped in the synagogue like any good Jew of the day, and it was not to abolish but to purify the Jerusalem temple that he so violently excoriated its commercialism. Although he was critical of some aspects of current religious patterns and practices, Judaism's scriptures and worship were the bedrock of his life, the context of his teaching, and the medium of his own personal experience and response to the love and will of God.

Far from being antinomian, then, Jesus at first glance appears to have been very much the traditionalist. He certainly cannot be cited as a justification for simply cutting one's self off from the past and venturing alone and unprepared into the future. For that matter, in his example today's Situation Ethic finds corroboration for its own insistence that previous experience and insights are a significant consideration in all ethical decision-making. And this is confirmed by Jesus' strong emphasis on the traditional Jewish law, and by the frequent definitive "thou shalts" and "thou shalt nots" that came from his lips. When asked by a rich young man what must be done to inherit eternal life, Jesus replied, "You know the commandments: 'Do not kill, Do not commit adultery, Do not steal, Do not bear false witness, Do not defraud, Honor your father and mother'" (Mk. 10:19). After healing a leper, he took pains to satisfy the Jewish law by commanding, "but go, show yourself to the priest, and offer for your cleansing what Moses commanded for a proof to the people" (Mk. 1:44). The Sermon on the Mount records many decisive and seemingly categorical pronouncements: "If your right eye causes you to sin, pluck it out and throw it away"; "Judge not, that you be not judged"; "You, therefore, must be perfect, as your heavenly Father is perfect" (Mt. 5:28, 7:1, 5:48).

Most familiar, perhaps, are those sayings in which Jesus explicitly commented upon the law of Moses in the form: "You have heard that it was said to the men of old. . . . But I say to you. . . ." (Mt. 5:21–48). For example, Moses held that, " 'whoever kills shall be liable to judgment.' But I say to you that every one who is angry with his brother shall be liable to judgment" (5:21, 22). According to the Ten Commandments, " 'You shall not commit adultery.' But I say to you that every one who looks at a woman lustfully has already committed adultery with her in his heart" (5:27, 28). In these and other such instances the obvious intent is not to cancel out the Mosaic commands, but by broadening and deepening them to underline their paramount importance as God's revealed will.

The legalist and the situationist alike affirm that if man believes in all humility that he can discern God's will obedience must follow. They agree, too, that biblical precepts are the embodiment of significant intimations about the divine will, and as such to be taken with high seriousness. Their disagreement is this: The legalist holds to the inviolability of these precepts, whereas the situationist insists that behind them lies *Agape,* and that in cases of conflict traditional biblical injunctions, such as the Ten Commandments, may, for that matter must, be disregarded. What can we say now about Jesus' position?

On the basis of what we have discovered thus far it would surely appear that his own attitude was closer to the legalist position. If further evidence is needed, these words are especially significant: "Think not that I have come to abolish the law and the prophets; I have come not to abolish them but to fulfill them. For truly, I say to you, till heaven and earth pass away, not an iota, not a dot, will pass from the law until all is accomplished. Whoever then relaxes one of the least of these commandments and teaches men so, shall be called least in the kingdom of heaven; but he who does them and teaches them shall be called great in the kingdom of heaven" (Mt. 5:17-19). In other words, not only the Ten Commandments, but the numerous other laws contained in the sacred scriptures and traditions of the Jewish people are of the greatest importance.

The Jesus of the gospels, then, to say the least, had a high regard for the revealed religious tradition of his people. One may wonder, at this point, how his authority could possibly be invoked to justify the situationist's categorical insistence that no law, however sacred, is immutable.

We have yet, however, to see these passages in their total context. Objectivity requires that we consider other sayings and actions of Jesus before coming to any final conclusions.

Especially important, for example, is the occasion when Jesus was asked by one of the scribes, "Which commandment is the first of all?" This was his immediate reply: "The first is, 'Hear, O Israel: The Lord our God, the Lord is one; and you shall love the Lord your God with all your heart, and with all your soul, and with all your mind, and with all your strength.' The second is this, 'You shall love your neighbor as yourself.' There is no other commandment greater than these" (Mk. 12:28-31; cf. Mt. 22:34-40, Lk. 10:25-28).

It is noteworthy here that in both parts of Jesus' injunction the same word, "love," is pivotal. That is, with these few words Jesus has embraced the whole of man's life and has indicated what that life "under God" is and does—and the single word *Agape* says it all. "Love," as St. Paul wrote, "is the fulfilling of [God's] law" (Rom. 13:10). And St. John, as we shall see, assumes and speaks at great length of the same vertical-horizontal pattern, with *Agape* the key to both parts:

"And this commandment we have from him, that he who loves God should love his brother also" (1 Jn. 4:21). This much, then, is clear: In the teaching of Jesus love occupied a cardinal position.

The crucial question, however, concerns the relationship between the injunction to love neighbor and the other precepts which Jesus is purported to have uttered. Today's Situation Ethic insists that *Agape* is not only important but that it has absolute priority over every other law. The more usual view, which holds that the other "do's" and "don'ts" promulgated by Holy Scripture are equally sacred, has tended rather to regard *Agape* as a kind of yeast which informs the whole. We are always, that is, to act as lovingly as possible, but it can never be a positive good to contravene these other specific biblical injunctions. What would Jesus have said to this?

We may take our cue from Mark 2:23–28. It was the sabbath. Jesus and a handful of his followers were walking through the fields. When the disciples became hungry they picked some ripe ears of grain and ate. A group of Pharisees who happened to observe what they did exclaimed, "Look, why are they doing what is not lawful on the sabbath?" (vs. 24). The objection was a petty one based on a technicality. To pluck grain was harvesting, harvesting was work, and all work on the sabbath was forbidden in accordance with the fourth of the Ten Commandments. Therefore Jesus, by raising no objection, had permitted his followers to break one of the most sacred laws given by God to Moses.

Jesus' reply to the Pharisees' well-meaning legalism (for such it was) opens up a whole new area for our consideration. "The sabbath," he said, "was made for man, not man for the sabbath" (vs. 27). These words are significant on two counts. For one thing, Jesus was appealing to what, centuries before, had been an important motivation behind the sabbath law's no-work clause, namely, a humane concern to provide each week one day of surcease from hard labor. As the years passed, the sabbath was enhanced with a theological significance which made the observance of a day of rest one of Judaism's most meaningful religious experiences. At the same time, there were many for whom the sabbath had come to be an end in itself. It had acquired so many restrictive regulations which caused inconvenience and hardship that the true purposes of the day, rest and worship, were largely negated.

This, then, was the particular problem against which Jesus' answer was directed, and it leads into a second and especially important point: More meaningful to Jesus than the sabbath law were the needs of people. The sabbath, an institution of high value both practically and theologically, and, according to the tradition, given by God through Moses (and we may be certain accepted as such and honored and observed by Jesus), was nevertheless a "thing," and the disciples were persons. In this particular situation, concern for their best good (*Agape*) dictated that the technicality of the law should be ignored. Here was a clear case of conflict between law and love. Jesus unhesitatingly chose the latter, because "the sabbath was made for man, and not man for the sabbath." In this instance *Jesus acted as a situationist!*

This particular story reaches its climax with the famous words, "so the Son of man is lord even of the sabbath" (vs. 28). Many biblical scholars think that we have here a later addition to Jesus' own words, and one which sought to interpret the story for those to whom it was told. The saying is indeed an apt summary, for it clearly and correctly explains that Jesus' actions and words were a rejection of rigid legalism. In Christ, the summary affirms, is the end of man's subservience to petty moralism and a new beginning of responsible freedom. Here, we may be certain, is reflected the actual experience of those who knew and followed Jesus during his earthly ministry. Not just this once, but continually the disciples had observed that his way with people was that of loving concern for their best good. More than this, his followers had experienced that "Christ-love" personally, because this had been his way with them. So it was that they came to understand the full significance of this memory of what happened on one particular sabbath. The story gives vivid expression to a fundamental tenet of Jesus' message: God's ultimate concern is not the preservation of codes, but persons and their needs.

This example is by no means unique. The gospels show that there were numerous occasions of controversy over the same issue between Jesus and the more correct orthodoxy of the Jewish religious leaders. These occurred because, impelled by an overriding concern for persons' greatest well-being, Jesus insisted upon "working," that is, healing or lending a helping hand on the sabbath day, thus repeatedly laying himself open to the charge of breaking the sacred fourth commandment.

An example of a different type is found in Mark 7:9–13. Here the conflict lay between a sacred oath (pledging an offering to the temple) and the need of one's parents (the fifth commandment: "honor your father and mother"). If a man who has vowed to make an offering to the temple is suddenly faced with his parents' unforeseen need and is forced by circumstances to choose between obligations, what should he do? Both were laws; each performed a valuable service. But Jesus did not hesitate. Even though the temple was holy it was a "thing"; an oath, even though made in God's name, was likewise a "thing." The parents were persons. Love in this situation dictated that their need had priority. Today's situationist would use the same criterion, and we may suspect in this particular instance come up with a similar conclusion. One wonders, incidentally, how many of the contributions that are made to churches or to various charities today are actually misplaced "conscience money," that is, a means of avoiding the direct personal action which loving concern demands whenever at all possible.

In the case under discussion, however, it might be proposed that we should attribute Jesus' decision simply to the fact that it satisfies one of the Ten Commandments. The account seems to go out of its way to contrast "the tradition of men" with "the commandment of God" (vss. 8, 9). That is, the law that regulates pledging to the temple is a matter of ecclesiastical legislation; it is good in the proper circumstance, but human in its conception and execution. In contrast, the precept for which Jesus opts comes from Moses and is no less than the very word of God himself (vs. 13), which is a very different matter indeed. We have already noted Jesus' deep reverence for the religious practices and precepts which he inherited, and here it could be argued is another case in point.

Nevertheless, it seems far preferable to understand Jesus' ultimate motivation as a deeper one. That is, he cited the fifth commandment not as an absolute never to be broken, but because in this particular instance obedience to the Mosaic injunction was the most loving thing to do. This is not to suggest that the commandment to honor one's parents is other than a highly salutary guideline. It would be a most exceptional circumstance indeed which would justify one's disregarding it. The point, rather, is that Jesus in the final analysis made his decision not as a protector of the law, but as a situationist and on the basis of *Agape*. This interpretation, for one thing, permits one to understand the incident in a manner consistent with the principle "law was made for man, not man for the law" which, as we have seen, led Jesus, on more than one occasion, to take the exceptional step of violating the sabbath law. Equally important, to see here loving concern for persons rather than fulfillment of the fifth commandment as the ultimate criterion is to construe Jesus' decision, and properly so, against the background of his ministry as a whole—a ministry that was characterized by a sensitivity to the needs of people which was so deep and compelling that it refused to be deterred by any barrier.

That this was so is vividly apparent in the following incident: "And as he sat at table in his house, many tax collectors and sinners were sitting with Jesus and his disciples; for there were many who followed him. And the scribes of the Pharisees, when they saw that he was eating with sinners and tax collectors, said to his disciples, 'Why does he eat with tax collectors and sinners?' " (Mk. 2:15, 16). The question from the standpoint of the religious purist was not without point. "Tax collectors and sinners" were, at the least, people to be viewed with suspicion. The former were especially despised because they served what were considered to be the unjust demands of Rome, the hated oppressor of the Jews. The term "sinners" was a catchall expression embracing all who were unable, or indifferent and unwilling, to obey the numerous complex religious prescriptions of the Judaism of that day. For Jesus to mingle with such individuals was to expose himself to the same ritual uncleanness (owing to technical violations of the religious law) which characterized these "sinners," and, in the familiar pattern of guilt by association, to lay himself open to malicious speculation and calumny.

Jesus' reply to the critical scribes and Pharisees sharply delineates the difference between legalism and *Agape*'s loving concern in action: "Those who are well have no need of a physician, but those who are sick; I came not to call the righteous, but sinners" (vs. 17). In other words, Jesus' concern was for people. His good news about God's love was for all. He could not answer their needs from a distance. For the sake of love he (who in a different situation told the healed leper to obey the law of ritual cleanness meticulously, Mark 1:44) broke the law—and often. His constant association with the outcasts of Jewish society was one of the most distinctive features of his ministry.

In the initial pages of this chapter we noted that the gospels, and especially that of St. Matthew, stress Jesus' role as a traditionalist and authoritative lawgiver. Now a more complete picture has emerged, and one that puts a different light on the matter. The Jesus who underlined the importance of the law and the prophets (Mt. 5:17–20) also condemned the Pharisee who had observed all the traditional precepts but did not love the Publican: "He also told this parable to some who trusted in themselves that they were righteous and despised others" (Lk. 18:9–14). Similarly he enjoined the upright young lawyer who had kept the commandments "from my youth" to "go, sell all that you have, and give it to the poor" (Mk. 10:17–22). That is, law without self-giving for others avails nothing. The Jesus who was so aware of the seriousness of sexual irresponsibility that he warned against looking at a woman lustfully (Mt. 5:28) nevertheless forgave a woman condemned to death by the law for committing adultery in order that she might rejoice in a new beginning (Jn. 8:3–11). He who categorically commanded that we should not retaliate evil for evil, that we bless those who persecute us, and that we love our enemies, nevertheless drove the money-changers out of the temple with a whip and employed the strongest possible invective against those religious leaders who idolized monetary gain and tradition to the detriment of people's needs. In other words, Jesus was thoroughly flexible with respect to those same sacred laws which his own words held in special reverence. Given what he considered to be the proper situation, he did not hesitate to place people and their needs before all else. And Christian situationists are asking today, "If Jesus himself did not treat the traditional precepts of a revealed religion as inviolable, why should we?"

We have now reached the point where we can better appreciate the position of those who claim the authority of Jesus himself for their insistence that love alone is the ultimate criterion for decision-making. Admittedly, proof positive that the claim is correct is impossible. The gospels do not offer examples of Jesus' contravening every law of his day. Furthermore, there is no record of his having discussed the matter of

laws versus absolutes, or of legalism versus freedom, in the
technical language of, or from the perspective of, today's Situation Ethic. And we most certainly cannot read his mind. We
have, nevertheless, uncovered certain elements of the gospel
picture which clearly underline the strength of the situationist's position. It is now apparent that Jesus himself understood
Agape not simply as one of many guidelines for man's relationship with others, but as something in a special category all
its own. There is no question but that he held the religious
laws of his tradition in high esteem. It is equally certain that
he did not hesitate to go beyond these laws. He did not do
this arbitrarily, but whenever and wherever a primary concern
for persons and sensitivity to human need dictated. Never, as
far as the gospel record is concerned, did he default from this
criterion, or allow any other consideration to have a higher
claim.

We have all been so conditioned by the popular use of the
word "love" that it is not easy to grasp the full weight and
richness of its biblical meaning. It is important to recognize
at the outset that "loving" and "liking" can be two very different things. We have already suggested in passing that *Agape*
is not a "feeling" but rather an attitude rooted in the will
which impels one to action. For this we may be grateful. If it
were otherwise few of us would ever bestir ourselves except by
fits and starts. Affection, as an emotion, cannot be commanded,
nor is compassion a reliable guide, because it is largely a conditioned response which varies from individual to individual.
Moreover, there are numerous needs waiting for love's minis-
tration which, either because of their remoteness or their
nature, do not appeal to one's personal tastes and so fail to
rouse the emotions of those who should be concerned.

Christian *Agape,* rather, depends upon recognizing that
herein lies a divine demand, taking one's self in hand, and,
through the use of will and determination and reliance upon

the grace of God, getting the job done quite apart from personal feelings for the task or for the individuals involved.
This, to be sure, is not the whole story. It is a remarkable
attribute of Christian experience that to pray and labor for
others often, as a later result, induces a meaningful emotional
involvement as well. It is also true that *Agape* points beyond
itself and provides ultimate rewards for the giver. This, too,
is an important part of the total Christian gospel—that man
must not only give, but must also, if life is to be complete,
receive. In its first beginnings, however, biblical love is a
willed movement toward another which enables one to act
strenuously for his neighbor's best good even when the recipient is thoroughly disliked. Our own pleasure, or lack of it, in
the act of loving is irrelevant.

For all this we find corroboration in the gospel picture of
Jesus. He appears to have been well aware of the difficulty of
loving others, because many of his words as recorded by the
Evangelists clearly point to *Agape*'s independence from emotion. This is suggested, for example, by the hard saying
recorded in the Sermon on the Mount: "You have heard that
it was said, 'You shall love your neighbor and hate your
enemy.' But I say to you, Love your enemies and pray for
those who persecute you. . . . For if you love those who love
you, what reward have you? Do not even the tax collectors do
the same? And if you salute only your brethren, what more
are you doing than others? Do not even the Gentiles do the
same?" (Mt. 5:43–47). Some perhaps may be able to "feel"
good will toward those who do them harm; but for most at
least, to love one's persecutors will not mean that we like
them. Moreover, it is not essential to the "doing" of *Agape*
that we should. Jesus' words here make it clear that love is
something demanded and possible even when there is no
positive emotional involvement.

The hard work which *Agape* requires is underlined by another saying reported by St. Matthew: "But I say to you, Do

not resist one who is evil. But if anyone strikes you on the right cheek, turn to him the other also; and if any one would sue you and take your coat, let him have your cloak as well; and if any one forces you to go one mile, go with him two miles" (5:39–41). These words, which employ the typical semitic teaching device of hyperbole, completely undercut any idea that Christian love depends upon one's emotional state. We can hardly imagine being overjoyed at the opportunity to be mistreated or robbed or persecuted. It would be silly to suggest that we need be. Moreover, Jesus' assertion that we should, as it were, "double the take" perhaps expresses his certainty that neither retaliation nor pious intoning of the eighth or tenth commandments ("Thou shalt not steal." "Thou shalt not covet."), but personal concern for the evildoer is the divinely willed response.

These same injunctions also make it clear that one's neighbors do not consist only of personal friends who happen to live more or less next door. In this connection the Parable of the Good Samaritan deserves special comment (Lk. 10:29–37). It is noteworthy that St. Luke locates this story immediately after Jesus' summary of the law in terms of love for God and neighbor. This suggests that the Evangelist records the parable for the specific purpose of demonstrating what Jesus meant by that *Agape* whose importance he has just proclaimed. In its present form, as commentators are fond of pointing out, the story shows signs of having undergone certain modifications. When first told by Jesus its purpose seems to have been the shaming of certain Jewish leaders by pointing out that a Samaritan, who was despised by the orthodox as a "half-Jew," had, nevertheless, managed to single out the thing of chief importance, namely, man's responsibility for his fellows. The priest and the Levite, on the other hand, who as religious authorities should have known that persons are more important than legal niceties, preferred to adhere to technicalities of

the law rather than rescue an indigent stranger who was
perhaps ritually "unclean." That is, the end result of a hard
and fast legalism is the closing of hearts which *Agape* keeps
open.

As it stands today, the parable is introduced with the question, "And who is my neighbor?" (vs. 29). These words, probably an addition to the story in its earlier form, give to the
whole a further significance which becomes apparent in the
next verse: "A man was going down from Jerusalem to
Jericho, and he fell among robbers, who stripped him and
beat him, and departed, leaving him half-dead" (vs. 30). The
anonymity of this poor unfortunate is significant. There is no
identification, not the slightest indication as to age, to race,
or to any other distinguishing feature. He is simply a man—
someone in trouble. Who is my neighbor? "Anyone," is the
reply, "not just those whom you know or happen to like, but
anyone and everyone who has need!"

According to the gospels, then, Jesus' attitude is clear:
"Liking" for an individual or a cause is completely irrelevant
to *Agape*'s task. To recognize this, it should be noted, is to
have the horizons of one's own obligation and potential effectiveness immeasurably enlarged. Herein lies a biblical foundation for the suggestion made in Chapter I that today's New
Morality, for all its sensationalism, has an underlying significance which is far greater than is usually recognized. Its true
imperative is Christian love. And that love, as we have seen,
speaks pointedly not merely to the private lives of individuals,
but with equal urgency to world-wide areas of contemporary
concern, thereby sharpening awareness of needs which hitherto
perhaps we have considered quite outside the boundaries of
our personal responsibility. *Agape* overrides all of the inhibiting superficial criteria of political persuasion, or race, or
religion, and also all of the presuppositions that we have
inherited from those before us. It is pleasant, indeed, to like

one's neighbors, but the Christian's chief prayer must be that he may receive the will and the power to love them.

To love the unlovely is especially difficult. And the Christian New Morality demands precisely this, a fact that dramatically belies any charge that it is soft or an easy way out of problem situations. Love of such a kind is hard work. *Agape* does not calculate beforehand whether or not there will be a response. It simply goes ahead, recognizing that in the needs of others there is for one's self a call and a vocation to service which supersede all else.

Not only have Jesus' sayings made all this clear. Equally significant for our consideration is the picture of his own life. More important than what people say is what they do, and the same is true of Jesus. When we examine his ministry with particular reference to his activities and his relationships with people, we can see new dimensions of that *Agape* of which he spoke. The picture of his life which unfolds is one of total self-giving for others. He was the servant of every person whom he encountered. His earthly existence was the unmistakable embodiment of his own injunction, "you shall love your neighbor." We must look at the picture in more detail.

Jesus had been active in Galilee for only a few weeks when John the Baptist sent a delegation from prison asking, "Who are you? Are you the Messiah expected by Judaism?" Jesus' reply is as important for what it omits as for what it includes: "Go and tell John what you hear and see: the blind receive their sight and the lame walk, lepers are cleansed and the deaf hear, and the dead are raised up, and the poor have good news [the reality of God's active concern and love] preached to them. And blessed is he who takes no offense at me" (Mt. 11:2–6; cf. Lk. 7:18–23). As to who he is, there is no specific answer. It is almost as if his own status is beside the point. What is important is not himself, but God, and recognition that God's own love in action has become a reality for many through his (Jesus') ministry. Wherever he has gone, with whomever he has come in contact, he has given all that he was and had, laboring for those in need by comforting, encouraging, healing, and, most important of all, evidencing his concern. "And blessed is he who takes no offense at me." These additional words, properly understood in the same vein, are not self-exaltation, but rather an encouragement to those able to discern in his demonstrable love for others the effectual working of God's own powerful concern for the world of men.

On almost every page of the gospels this picture of one who lived only to serve others is confirmed. To Zacchaeus, a tax collector who had grown rich from the graft of his trade, Jesus called out, "Zacchaeus, make haste and come down [out of that tree]; for I must stay at your house today" (Lk. 19:5); and as a result Zacchaeus became a new person. Jesus allowed a prostitute to anoint and kiss his feet, and lifted from her shoulders the guilt of a wretched past: "Your sins are forgiven" (Lk. 7:48). With loving hands he touched the sick who crowded around him, and the result was healing, and with the new wholeness came new hope. He cared about people who were physically hungry because he was concerned for their bodies as well as for their souls: "I have compassion on the crowd" (Mk. 8:2). And he responded, not because they were pious or might become so, but simply because they were persons and in need of food. He cared about the needs of his disciples and their families, and told them where most successfully they might cast their nets for fish (Lk. 5:1–11). In all of this activity Jesus reminds one of his own Parable of the Marriage Feast in which the king sent out his servants to invite (St. Luke says "compel") people to attend (Mt. 22:1–14; Lk. 14:16–24). But in real life it was Jesus himself who as the servant of all went out and searched the highways and byways of Galilee and Judaea, seeking the lost, eating with sinners, and, as an equal among equals, rubbing shoulders with the dirty and the unkempt and the unlovely. And somehow through his own self-giving he imparted to many that without which life simply makes no sense—the assurance that someone cared for them, just as they were and with no ulterior motive, and as well the joyful realization that their lives were important, and that the future was not without meaning and hope after all.

One of the most humorous and, at the same time, saddest stories in the gospels is that which is related in Luke 22:24–30. It was the eve of Jesus' death and the time of the Last Supper. During the meal (according to St. Luke this happened just after Jesus had shared the bread and cup as an anticipatory self-humbling on their behalf through his death!), "A dispute also arose among [the disciples], which of them was to be regarded as the greatest." How Jesus must have felt it is difficult to imagine. They had been with him constantly for many weeks, had heard his words, had seen his love at work, and still they did not understand that to obey God's command to love means to surrender all claims for self. And on this night of all nights they fought among themselves over rank and positions of preferment.

For the last time, therefore, Jesus sought to make clear what love is and does. In the gentile world, he began, kings and benefactors receive honor and plaudits. "But," he continued, "not so with you; rather let the greatest among you become as the youngest, and the leader as one who serves" (vs. 26). Then, using their own table fellowship of the moment as an example, he asked, "For which is the greater, one who sits at table, or one who serves? Is it not the one who sits at table? *But I [who sit here with you] am among you as one who serves*" (vs. 27). These final words offer a superb summary description of the shape of Jesus' entire ministry. They depict, as well, his ensuing death. He went to Calvary still as the servant of others, trusting that through the cross, no less than through his day by day self-giving, love's power to create new persons would have its way.

When the Situation Ethic speaks of love, it is recalling the servant life of Jesus the Christ who died on Calvary now almost two thousand years ago.

It cannot be overstated, because the popular misconception on this point is colossal: There is nothing soft or sentimental about that love which lies at the heart of the Christian New Morality. *Agape* is not self-seeking, but self-giving. If there are any lingering doubts about this it should be noted that Jesus was the *suffering* servant of God (whose will he refused to disobey) and of man. Inevitably, to love totally and to insist upon carrying such love into action will bring moments of pain. Denying one's self, as we well know, is always a struggle. If Gethsemane has any meaning, it must have been so for Jesus, too. More than this, in a world which is imperfect because it is still in process of creation, love for others will often receive no self-satisfying response; on the contrary, it will frequently meet with unpopularity, rejection, and even persecution. The chief symbol (and strength) of *Agape* is the cross of Calvary; and Jesus' acceptance of its utter dereliction underlines as can nothing else love's absolute priority in his own life. So all-important is love's imperative that it is worth the ultimate in self-denial. Nothing could be more clear: Christian love (and hence the Christian New Morality) is neither selfish nor indulgent; here, rather, is the stuff that makes martyrs.

The gospel picture stresses this throughout. Long before he was crucified, Jesus knew that the servant life to which he had been called might well entail personal tragedy. The Evangelists tell us that initially some hearers were impressed with his teaching and his ability to heal. Nevertheless, there soon developed increasing friction between Jesus and the more orthodox leaders of Judaism. His constant concern in action for the undesirables of the Palestinian social structure, his ready mingling with them, his willingness to disregard convention and law whenever need demanded, all made him suspect.

There was a further complication. The Roman conquerors of Palestine, as personified by the procurator Pontius Pilate and the tetrarch Herod Antipas, were alarmed by Jesus' activity. They feared that his popularity in some quarters would stir those already restless under severe foreign oppression into open rebellion. Not long before, John the Baptist, who had obtained a considerable following with his own preaching of repentance and judgment, had been executed, most likely, as the Jewish historian Flavius Josephus suggests, for political reasons rather than because he made certain barbed and perhaps deserved remarks about Herod's latest matrimonial venture (Mk. 6:18). Many hints in the gospels make it clear that Jesus was aware of all these factors. He knew that opposition was growing, and along with it serious risk for himself.

The Evangelists Matthew, Mark, and Luke all bring this out into the open with their accounts of Peter's open acclamation of Jesus as the Messiah at Caesarea Philippi (Mk. 8:27–33; Mt. 16:13–23; Lk. 9:18–22). Jesus' response on this occasion is especially significant. As St. Mark relates it, "he charged them to tell no one about him. And he began to teach them that the Son of man must suffer many things, and be rejected by the elders and the chief priests and the scribes, and be killed. . . . And he said this plainly. And Peter took him, and began to rebuke him. But turning and seeing his disciples, he rebuked Peter, and said, 'Get behind me, Satan! For you are not on the side of God, but of men' " (Mk. 8:30–33).

Underlying these words is Jesus' clear recognition that the combination of forces operating against him spelled out personal disaster. If he persisted in upsetting the status quo by such total living of all that love is and does, he would be killed. Peter's attempt to rebuke his master is also significant. It shows that, despite an intuitive sense that in this Jesus they had encountered a marvel unique in their experience, the disciples were still far from understanding the deep meaning of his life: Love is central, and its uninhibited exercise inevitably involves risk for one's self. The unseemly squabbling over personal status at the time of the Last Supper indicates that even at the end they still had not gotten the point.

St. Mark records another saying which underlines love's hardship, not only for Jesus, but for all who accept his way as their own. "Are you able," he asked James and John, "to drink the cup that I drink, or to be baptized with the baptism with which I am baptized?" (Mk. 10:38). These words are a metaphorical reference to suffering, and the two disciples glibly answered, "We are able." Jesus then assured them that such would indeed be their vocation. There is no escaping the reality that denial of self for God and man is a hard and narrow road: "If any man would come after me, let him deny himself and take up his cross and follow me" (Mk. 8:34). Jesus' understanding and expectation are clear. *Agape* is not motivated by personal gratification. It is impelled by a divine call and anticipates unresponsiveness and seeming failure. Nevertheless, it will endure any difficulty if in that way it can answer the needs of others. Such is the love which Christ the suffering servant lays upon his followers as the essential pattern of their lives and of their discipleship.

To be sure, we cannot be certain; the information available to us is too slight. But there is reason to believe that had Jesus been more circumspect, less abandoned in his concern for others, the end result might have been different. *Agape,* however, is not cautious when it comes to self, not at least when one accepts, as did Christ, that here is a divine imperative. When it became apparent to Jesus that the way led to total self-surrender in death, he knew love's full agony and prayed in Gethsemane that he might, after all, be spared: "Father, if thou art willing, remove this cup from me"; but he did not falter: "nevertheless, not my will, but thine, be done" (Lk. 22:42). He even suffered the most crushing experience of all, the momentary wonder if perhaps everything that he had said and done had been a waste, and the despair of feeling that no one, not even God, cared: "My God, my God, why hast thou forsaken me?" (Mt. 27:46). "For the Son of man also came not to be served but to serve, and to give his life as a ransom for many" (Mk. 10:45). This is Christian love! This is the love which motivates the Christian New Morality!

The Apostle Paul commented upon Jesus' servant life with these words, "For you know the grace of our Lord Jesus Christ, that though he was rich, yet for your sake he became poor, so that by his poverty you might become rich" (2 Cor. 8:9). On another occasion he defined that love more specifically: "Love does not insist on its own way. . . . Love bears all things, believes all things, hopes all things, endures all things" (1 Cor. 13:4–7). The author of the Epistle to the Hebrews wrote: "For we have not a high priest who is unable to sympathize with our weaknesses, but one who in every respect has been tempted as we are, yet without sinning" (Heb. 4:15). Jesus himself, St. John tells us, after having summed up the meaning of his entire life by assuming the menial task of washing his disciples' feet, enjoined, "Greater love has no man than this, that a man lay down his life for his friends" (Jn. 15:13).

When the Christian New Morality says, "nothing matters but love," this is the kind of love of which it speaks. When the Christian situationist says, "Not what I please, but what Christ pleases," it is to this kind of self-denying and self-giving concern in action that he refers. In the final analysis, it is not certain chance words of Jesus but, far more important and compelling, his verifiable servant life and death which make the New Morality's claim to dominical authority so impressive.

Before we leave the gospel story, this fundamental question

is of special importance: *Why* did Jesus love so fully? and
whence came the will and the strength for such complete self-
giving? One simple answer, which is correct enough as far as
it goes, would be this: He believed that the injunction to love
neighbor was a divine command, and he obeyed it. However,
it will be profitable to look more closely.

Jesus' key summary of what a man's life should be and do,
we must remember, contained two injunctions. Thus far we
have concerned ourselves almost entirely with the second:
"you shall love your neighbor." Equally important is that
which precedes it: "you shall love the Lord your God." For
Jesus, to love God meant to acknowledge the divine sovereignty as total and absolute, and without reserve to surrender
one's self to it. And, as is dramatically illustrated by the
account of the temptation in the wilderness that foreshadows
his entire ministry, there was nothing more characteristic of
Jesus' own life than precisely this awareness and humble acceptance of God's "allness": "You shall worship the Lord your
God, and him only shall you serve" (Mt. 4:10; Lk. 4:8).

In these last words, however, side by side with self-sub-
mission ("worship") stands the call to obedience ("serve"). The
biblical imagery of kingship, it is helpful to remember, was
conditioned by a familiarity with oriental potentates, whose
every word and gesture were law. God is King, and not in
name only, but in full reality. To place one's self in God's
hands is to bow to the sovereign will. And once again the
fundamental pattern is evident. According to Jesus' teaching
and servant life, the King's will is succinctly summarized in
the command to love neighbor. And for Jesus, to love God is
to obey God, and the two injunctions of his summary constitute one indivisible whole cloth. The implication seems clear,
and one which, as we shall see, St. John boldly makes explicit:
It's all or nothing—love for others is an inevitable concomi-
tant of love for God. Here, then, we see something of the
"why" of Jesus' servanthood. But there is more.

For Jesus, God was King and also God was Father. Actually, Jesus appears to have employed the latter term much more frequently, and in his teaching the concept of divine father-hood received an emphasis and attained a significance hitherto unknown. Again, it is important to recall the contemporary context of this imagery. Within a Jewish family the father was an authoritative figure who commanded and received obedience. At the same time, he was one whose concern and personal self-giving for his dependents and their needs were paramount. Such, said Jesus, is God, "our Father," one who not only demands, but who also wills to give and sustain and make whole. So, for example, God is one who will "give good things to those who ask him" (Mt. 7:7–11). Even for the un-worthy, and for those who know him not, he provides: "for he makes his sun rise on the evil and on the good, and sends rain on the just and on the unjust" (Mt. 5:45). He is aware of man's needs, and knows that these are important: "But if God so clothes the grass of the field . . . will he not much more clothe you, O men of little faith?" (Mt. 6:30). The Parable of the Prodigal Son is a picture of the kind of for-giveness which God exercises (Lk. 15:11–32). In the parables of the Lost Sheep and the Lost Coin, God is depicted as one who yearningly seeks his own (Lk. 15:3–10). Examples such as these could be multiplied many times. They all proclaim that God is himself one who gives, and that to submit to his king-ship is to know not only his demand, but as well the joy and the power of his love.

Herein we can see another and deeper reason for Jesus' servant life and death. To submit to God's kingship is to know that his is a sovereignty of love. To love God is, as never be-fore, to become aware of God's love for one's self, and to be seized by it. For Jesus, then, to do God's will involved more than mere mechanical obedience to a command. Rather, Jesus was the servant of man because he so rejoiced in God's love for himself. Here is something that we can understand from

our own imperfect human experience—the irresistible longing
to please (to do the will of) the one whose love we welcome
for ourselves. Again, St. John's Gospel expresses it most
clearly: "As the Father has loved me, so have I loved you"
(Jn. 15:9).

All this further underlines that love for others is inescapably
a part of love for God. Truly to let God reign in one's life is
to know a joy of self-acceptance which impels one, in willing
answer to God's call, to share the divine love with others.
Such is the significance of Jesus' servant life which found both
the will and the strength to spend itself through its utter
abandonment to God's own love.

To love God is to love one's neighbor. St. Paul and St.
John, each in his own way, make much of this, as we shall see.
For the moment, we may be content with one important
observation: The seemingly flippant slogan of the New Morality, "nothing matters but love," has a depth of which few are
aware. In both parts of Jesus' summary, *Agape*—love in the
sense of self-giving—is the key word. Such love is meant to
motivate, to embrace, to fulfill the totality of a man's life:
love God, love others. Clearly, whatever individuals may conclude about its current speculations, the Situation Ethic is a
significant attempt to interpret both the teaching and the
person of Jesus. The Christian love, which it seeks to apply
to today's world, is no mere impulse of sentimental good will.
It is an imperative which receives its authorization and drive
from the very depths of Christian discernment, and from the
experience of the God who has revealed himself through
Christ.

III

Saint Paul: Faith Active in Love

St. Paul, servant of Jesus Christ and Apostle to the Gentiles, may never have seen Jesus during his earthly ministry. It is certain that he was not one of the original disciples. His conversion to Christianity, for that matter, came only after a period of several years, during which time he was an active persecutor of the tiny Christian church. For all his earlier hostility, however, once he had become Christ's man he seized upon the central point of Jesus' ethical teaching with sureness. Nothing could be clearer than these words written to a colony of Christians residing in the great imperial city of Rome: "Owe no one anything, except to love one another; for he who loves his neighbor has fulfilled the law. The commandments, 'You shall not commit adultery, You shall not kill, You shall not steal, You shall not covet,' and any other commandment, are summed up in this sentence, 'You shall love your neighbor as yourself.' Love does no wrong to a neighbor; therefore love is the fulfilling of the law" (Rom. 13:8–10).

This exhortation, so obviously reminiscent of Jesus' own

summary of the law in terms of *Agape* (Mk. 12:28–31), speaks for itself. Adherents of the Situation Ethic need not rely solely upon the gospels in their search for scriptural evidence. In this and in the following chapter, we shall see that not only St. Paul but the early church as a whole "got the message." This does not mean that all, or even most early Christians fully understood, or lived up to love's demands perfectly. There were legalists in those days as well as now and, at the opposite pole, there were misguided antinomians who recognized no ethical responsibility of any kind. Nevertheless, the repeated stress upon *Agape* throughout the New Testament lends significant weight to the New Morality's claim that it does not advocate a novel departure, but rather poses the imperative necessity of accepting with new seriousness a basic premise of earliest Christianity.

St. Paul, to return to his letters, not only correctly discerned the core of Jesus' ethical teaching, but he also went straight to the heart of Jesus' ministry, and especially of his death. The Jesus of the gospels, to a unique degree, lived that servant life which he insisted to be God's will for all. This, St. Paul thoroughly understood, and he shared with his contemporaries the sure conviction that the wonderful newness that had transformed their lives had been the direct result of that same Christ-love. Explain it how one might (and the New Testament is rich with meaningful attempts to this end), they knew that somehow, and wonderfully, it was Jesus Christ who had made the difference. It was as though he had been the personal servant of each one of them. "You were bought with a price," St. Paul writes, because "Christ died for our sins in accordance with the scriptures"; "But God shows his love for us in that while we were yet sinners Christ died for us"; "and the life I now live in the flesh I live by faith in the Son of God, who loved me and gave himself for me" (1 Cor. 6:20, 7:23, 15:3; Rom. 5:8; Gal. 2:20). In such manner the first believers, compelled by the joy which they knew had been effected by his coming into their lives, pointed to Jesus' servanthood and climactic death as an action of love for their best good, and for the good of the whole world.

St. Paul's most striking reference to the servant Christ occurs in his letter to the Philippians: "who, though he was in the form of God, did not count equality with God a thing to be grasped, but emptied himself, taking the form of a servant, being born in the likeness of men. And being found in human form he humbled himself and became obedient unto death, even death on a cross" (Phil. 2:6–8). The correspondence between this description and our reference in the previous chapter to Jesus' own understanding of his mission and of its cost ("I am among you as one who serves"; "For the Son of man . . . came . . . to serve, and to give his life as a ransom for many"; Lk. 22:27, Mk. 10:45) needs little comment. Paul had indeed gotten the point: Jesus was one for whom love was paramount.

This particular passage from the Epistle to the Philippians has understandably played a significant part in the history of doctrine during those long years when the church's deepening awareness of Christ's uniqueness impelled her theologians to explain the ultimate reality of Jesus of Nazareth in terms of divinity. St. Paul's own immediate interest in these words, however, was quite different. His primary concern was not "theology," but the moving description of the earthly Jesus' obedience to God and his humble love for others. Here, he is saying, is the divinely revealed pattern and source of power for all Christians in their daily lives. This is clearly indicated by the words with which the passage is introduced: "Let your bearing towards one another arise out of your life in Christ Jesus" (vs. 5, NEB). A bit further on he, in effect, repeats the exhortation: "So you too, my friends, must be obedient, as always" (vs. 12, NEB). That is, Christian living means obedience to the divine will (love God) as it has been revealed in

Christ's own servant love (love neighbor). The Apostle's Christ was the servant Christ, and herein, for all to see, was made plain God's way for every man.

To love God is to love others. For Jesus, as we have seen, this meant that *Agape* is the ultimate criterion for every action and for every relationship. This, too, St. Paul understood. Let us look at a case in point taken from his own pastoral experience. We shall follow his thinking in some detail, because this particular matter not only demonstrates his own clear stance as a situationist, but also illustrates the carefully reasoned manner that a situationist generally must use in his attempts to determine what *Agape* demands.

The specific problem which evoked the Apostle's concern is discussed at length in 1 Corinthians 8:1–11:1. Is it right and proper, he had been asked, for a Christian to eat meat which has been previously consecrated to pagan idols? A strange question indeed from our viewpoint. At that time, however, some of the "fresh" meat sold in the open market places had previously been dedicated at pagan religious ceremonies. One never knew (nor did non-Christians care) whether he was eating such holy food or not, and some of Paul's converts were perplexed. If perchance such consecrated meat was consumed by a Christian, did this in any way associate the believer with idol worship, and thus compromise his loyalty to the one God?

Some, including St. Paul himself, saw no special problem here, at least theoretically. The Apostle replied to inquiries from the church in Corinth: "Hence, as to the eating of food offered to idols, we know that 'an idol has no real existence,' and that 'there is no God but one'" (1 Cor. 8:4). In other words, because there is only one God, food consecrated to non-existent deities has no possible sacred significance for the Christian. Therefore he is free to eat what he pleases: "Eat whatever is sold in the meat market without raising any question on the ground of conscience" (1 Cor. 10:25). Besides,

"Food will not commend us to God. We are no worse off if we do not eat, and no better off if we do" (1 Cor. 8:8). This would seem to end the matter.

St. Paul, however, had more to say. Right knowledge or theology ("there is no God but one") is a fine thing to have; but what if "not all possess this knowledge" (1 Cor. 8:7)? Paul, that is, knows of certain Christians whose consciences in this matter still troubled them. Some perhaps were more recent converts from paganism who had not yet apprehended the full implications of their new faith. Many, moreover, still believed in the existence of various lesser supernatural spirits who were sometimes associated with pagan deities. Possibly there were others who were simply concerned lest any seeming participation in idol worship compromise the Christian witness to pagan non-believers. In any event, the Apostle was aware that there were circumstances which demanded caution. And not least was the danger that eating on the part of those more knowledgeable in the presence of those less knowledgeable would cause confusion and scandal within the Christian community itself. Some who were its members might well suffer anxiety, a deep sense of guilt, or even the loss of faith.

What, then, did this situation demand? What criterion of decision should be employed? St. Paul did not hesitate. Here was an instance of conflict between right knowledge (theology) and the best good of persons. Without in any sense surrendering the theological point or denying its importance, he immediately focused upon the needs of people as the chief thing of the moment. That these "weaker" brethren were technically in error was beside the point. They were persons for whom Christ had died; and that love, which the cross proclaimed, must alone be the final determiner of one's actions. The knowledgeable Christian, for all his right theology, is bound to deny himself; he must use his freedom not as license for self-gratification, but in the context of that love which recognizes its responsibility for one's neighbor. "Only take care," the Apostle warns, "lest this liberty of yours somehow become a stumbling-block to the weak. For if any one sees you, a man of knowledge, at table in an idol's temple, might he not be encouraged, if his conscience is weak, to eat food offered to idols? And so by your knowledge this weak man is destroyed, the brother for whom Christ died. Thus, sinning against your brethren and wounding their conscience when it is weak, you sin against Christ. Therefore, if food is a cause of my brother's falling, I will never eat meat, lest I cause my brother to fall" (1 Cor. 8:9–13). In the Epistle to the Romans St. Paul writes about food problems in general: "If your brother is being injured by what you eat, you are no longer walking in love. Do not let what you eat cause the ruin of one for whom Christ died . . . it is right not to . . . do anything that makes your brother stumble" (Rom. 14:15–21).

The circumstances to which St. Paul addresses his remarks are so foreign to us that many regard this particular discussion in 1 Corinthians as simply irrelevant for a modern Christian. Actually, it is astonishingly contemporary, as we find are many other puzzling sections of the Bible, when we dig beneath the surface. The passage lays before the reader the very heart of the Christian gospel, namely, that love is the pivotal signification of Jesus' death and is likewise the primary demand laid upon his followers. Whatever the circumstances, and in whatever century or culture, here is a criterion for action that does not change. It is because of this, and because St. Paul correctly uses *Agape* as his decision-making principle, that this curious business has no less significance now than it did in the sixth decade of the first century. Moreover, his sensitivity in handling the matter is an excellent illustration of that which the Situation Ethic today posits as its basic methodology—love applied with reason. That is, the decisive criterion must always be *Agape*. And determining what *Agape* demands in any given situation requires the most comprehensive and intelligent assessment possible of all of the factors involved.

Paul's introduction to this problem includes these cautioning words: " 'Knowledge' puffs up, but love builds up" (1 Cor. 8:1). Elsewhere he asserts, "And if I have prophetic powers, and understand all mysteries and all knowledge, and if I have all faith, so as to remove mountains, but have not love, I am nothing" (1 Cor. 13:2). These words could just as easily have come from the lips of the servant Christ himself!

We must look at other facets of St. Paul's life and teaching. His discernment of *Agape* as the fundamental principle of Jesus' human existence, and his understanding of the ensuing implications for a Christian's every day activities, played an important role in shaping his own career. Furthermore, to a greater extent than is generally recognized, *Agape* was an essential ingredient in the formulation of several of those significant religious insights for which he is so well known. A careful examination of his many letters throws much light upon what it is that the Christian New Morality means and seeks to do in our time.

As a beginning, it will be helpful to sketch the process by which the Apostle came to recognize *Agape*'s pre-eminence. He tells us that in his pre-Christian days he had been a firm legalist: "circumcized on the eighth day, of the people of Israel, of the tribe of Benjamin, a Hebrew born of Hebrews; as to the law a Pharisee, as to zeal a persecutor of the church, as to righteousness under the law blameless" (Phil. 3:5, 6). Paul, that is, scrupulously adhered to those same precepts contained in the Old Testament and in the traditions of Judaism which we noted in the previous chapter. The law, with all its details, was precious to Judaism. Many believed that to accomplish all its demands was a sure way to win God's favour, attain present joy, and win ultimate salvation. St. Paul had shared this view, believing that the one thing demanded of him was that he measure up to all of the law's complex "do's" and "don'ts"; and he appears to have been at least moderately successful: "and I advanced in Judaism beyond many of my own age among my people, so extremely zealous was I for the traditions of my fathers" (Gal. 1:14).

At the same time, it is clear that life under the law left him dissatisfied: "the very commandment [law] which promised life proved to be death to me" (Rom. 7:10). That is, specific "thou shalts" and "thou shalt nots" seemed (a phenomenon not unfamiliar to us) only to make their opposites more attractive: "I should not have known what it is to covet if the law had not said, 'You shall not covet'" (Rom. 7:7). Even though he conformed to the law, joy was somehow lacking. Paul's inner self was torn and frustrated.

Then came his sudden conversion. The Book of Acts indicates that this traumatic event occurred while he was on his way to Damascus, still zealously hostile toward Christianity and planning to persecute members of the new sect in that city (Acts 9:1–9; 22:6–11; 26:12–18). What happened as far as details are concerned remains a source of endless and largely fruitless speculation, except for this one certainty—Paul was overwhelmed and won over by the Christ whom he had hitherto rejected, and from that moment on was his devoted slave. God, he writes, "called me through his grace, was pleased to reveal his Son to me" (Gal. 1:15, 16).

The word "grace" in this text is especially significant. In St. Paul's letters it means virtually the same thing as *Agape*. It bespeaks the kind of love that cares and gives and forgives and acts for another quite without regard for the recipient's merit or deserving. Paul, frustrated within Judaism and a persecutor of Christians, suddenly found himself a new person. He knew that what had happened to him on the Damascus road occurred through no conscious effort on his part, and almost despite himself; it certainly had nothing to do with

pleasing God through successful accomplishment of the multi-
tudinous works demanded by the law. It was God's love that
had seized him; his sudden new life was a sheer gift of grace
freely given to one totally unworthy. He summed it up this
way: "Last of all, as to one untimely born, [Christ] appeared
also to me. For I am the least of the apostles, unfit to be called
an apostle, because I persecuted the church of God. But by
the grace of God [and for no other reason] I am what I am,
and his grace toward me was not in vain" (1 Cor. 15:8–10).

So it was that St. Paul commenced a new life of freedom
from the law. At last he knew—and here again is a conviction
of the highest importance for the contemporary Situation
Ethic—that more important than any law, however sacred,
was God's love! Immediately we recall that this was the view
of Jesus himself. When, for example, he stated that "the sabbath was made for man," thereby underlining the traditional
day of rest as something graciously given by God for man's
best good, and refusing wooden adherence to regulations
which inhibited this purpose, he too was affirming the priority
of God's concern for the needs of persons over even the most
sacred laws of Judaism. In a similar manner St. Paul finally
rejected domination by tense and nervous straining to adhere
to the detailed mandates of his earlier legalism. The deeper
significance of what had happened must have taken him
months, even years, to understand; the results of his attempt
will, in part, become apparent in the pages that follow. But
it all began with the conversion experience which shifted the
focal point of Paul's entire life. The law, even though it was
the express will of God himself revealed to Moses on Mt.
Sinai, was relegated to a secondary role. Suddenly, and wonderfully, love had been given the priority.

St. Paul found that he had become a new person. Of what,
however, did this new life consist? God's love had freed him
from slavery to the principle of law; but what was to take

the law's place that would henceforth give coherence, purpose, and meaning to his existence? The Apostle's answer was
"faith." He states in a typical passage, "For Christ ends the
law and brings righteousness for everyone who has faith"
(Rom. 10:4, NEB).

More specifically, however, what is meant by "faith"? Who
or what is its object? Does it just "exist" in a kind of vacuum?
Is it an attitude, an activity, or what? Failure in the past to
give these questions careful consideration has often caused
serious misreading of Paul's understanding of the Christian
life. Furthermore, it continues to be a negative influence upon
Christian witness in the world.

The Apostle speaks most directly and clearly to these questions in Galatians 5:6: "For in Christ Jesus neither circumcision nor uncircumcision is of any avail, but faith working
through love." The introductory "in Christ Jesus" is a favorite
Pauline phrase with many rich implications which we shall
consider later. Its use here at the beginning of verse 6 underlines that what follows represents the distinctively Christian
stance as opposed to other viewpoints. One such opposing
view is indicated by the negative reference to "circumcision."
With these words Paul rejects the works of the Jewish law as
a means of salvation. For the Christian, it is affirmed, the very
principle of law (circumcision or uncircumcision—whatever
the law may be) is invalid. That which replaces law as the
center of one's life is "faith"—but not faith alone. St. Paul
very pointedly qualifies his reference: "faith *working through
love.*"

The italicized words in this important final phrase do not
bring out the full weight of the original Greek in which the
epistle was written. The New English Bible reads "faith
active in love"; that is, faith is something dynamic, constantly
on the move. It does not exist merely for itself, but is outgoing,
outgiving. This is best suggested by the J. B. Phillips trans-
lation, "faith *which expresses itself* in love." More than this,

even, faith realizes its potential, comes into its own, becomes a powerful and effectual reality in an individual's life *only* as it expresses itself in *Agape*.

Faith and love, then, are related in the closest possible way. And yet, more precisely, what does Paul mean by these two words? In this connection, the importance of the introductory phrase "in Christ Jesus" is again apparent. It makes clear that the Apostle is not speaking of faith and love in general, but of Christian faith and of Christian love, which means that in each instance the role of Christ is pivotal. Here, that is, as throughout his letters, faith means personal surrender of self in trust to the God who has been revealed by Jesus Christ. And by love he means that self-giving concern for others which the earthly Jesus' words and actions so plainly proclaimed and exemplified as God's will for all. In short, the expression "faith working through love" is a brilliant and accurate summary of Christ's own existence as depicted in the gospels: Jesus the servant of God and the servant of man. The Christian life, Paul affirms, is the very life of Christ himself—he for whom faith and love for others (love God, love neighbor) were inseparably one.

On a very practical level, what does all this mean? The Epistle of St. James affords an interesting illustration. The writer was distressed over specific instances of snobbishness and neglect exhibited by certain individuals of his acquaintance toward lesser members of the same Christian community. "You pay attention," he remarks, "to the one who wears the fine clothing and say, 'Have a seat here, please,' while you say to the poor man, 'Stand there,' or 'Sit at my feet' " (Jas. 2:3). "If," he remarks a few verses later, "you really fulfill the royal law, according to the scripture, 'You shall love your neighbor as yourself,' you do well" (2:8). Because, however, there are so many who fail in this regard, James is forced to add, "What does it profit, my brethren, if a man says he has faith but has not works? Can his faith save him? If a brother or sister is

ill-clad and in lack of daily food, and one of you says to them,
'Go in peace, be warmed and filled,' without giving them the
things needed for the body, what does it profit? *So faith by
itself, if it has no works, is dead"* (2:14–17).

St. Paul could not have said it better himself!

We have already hinted that St. Paul's concept of faith has
often been misunderstood. Most frequently, perhaps, the misreading has expressed itself in the slogan "faith *versus* works."
In one sense this phrase is correct enough. The Apostle does
insist that humble self-surrender to God's love, rather than
prideful attempts to extort God's favor by "doing good," is
the Christian way. And it is true that he often speaks of faith
as a single entity without specific reference to the love that it
impels. Many, however, have assumed this to mean that
faith, if not completely antithetical, is at least superior to
works, and the result is that works, at best, are regarded as
peripheral and secondary. Such a conclusion with respect to
Paul's intent is totally wrong. "Faith *and* works"—this is the
Pauline doctrine. Any other reading not only ignores the
inseparability of faith and love stressed in Galatians 5:6, but
also overlooks much else in the Apostle's letters.

Even during St. Paul's own lifetime there were apparently
those who used his words as justification for denigrating the
Christian ethical concern. He tells us about this in Romans
3:5–8 and 6:1. If, it was contended, faith is all that matters
(an "if" which ignored Paul's total understanding of the concept), and God in his graciousness continuously loves and forgives, in the final analysis what a man does with his daily life
is of no particular account. More than this, the argument
continues, since you, Paul, affirm that "our wickedness serves
to show the justice of God," why not, then, "do evil that
good may come?" (Rom. 3:5, 8). In other words, inasmuch as
the more we sin the more we are forgiven, our sinning can be
construed as a positive good which enhances the Deity because

it shows how magnanimous and merciful God really is. Practically speaking, then, loving concern for neighbor is not especially important. If one but has faith in God, he is free to please himself wherever fancy may lead.

This line of reasoning, of course, is fallacious. It completely ignores proper methodological procedure, which in this instance requires that St. Paul's comments on faith be interpreted not piecemeal, but against the backdrop of all that he wrote, and with regard for his personal life as well. This, however, his misinterpreters failed to do. Instead, as so often happens today when people are challenged by a controversial issue or person, they simply seized upon certain seemingly isolated dramatic statements and drew hasty conclusions without concern for the context in which they were spoken or written. Actually, one has but to flip through the pages of Paul's letters, in which time and again he pleads, threatens, rebukes, and exhorts his readers to proper concern active in well-doing for others, in order to see how seriously he views the Christian ethical obligation.

One of the Apostle's most effective rebuttals to those who misrepresented his view of faith appears in Romans 6:12–7:6. The passage is too long to quote here, but the substance of his reply is unmistakable. Before we became Christians, he reminds his readers, we were slaves to the law; but now we are free. And yet we must remember how we attained this freedom. It was given to us by Christ, and ours is the life in Christ. Actually, then, we have merely exchanged masters; our freedom from the law has become a new bondage to Christ. He writes, "Likewise, my brethren, you have died to the law through the body [that is, the death] of Christ, so that you may belong to another, to him who has been raised from the dead in order that we may bear fruit for God" (Rom. 7:4).

In this passage and throughout St. Paul's letters, Jesus Christ is central and key. Again we recall Galatians 5:6 where we noted the pivotal role played by the phrase "in Christ Jesus." For the believer, Christ is the measure of all that one is and does, and only against this background can the expression "faith working through love" be properly understood. In short, St. Paul's doctrine of faith cannot be isolated from the person of Christ, and it is the failure to take this adequately into account that, more than anything else, has led to the misleading slogan "faith versus works" and its misuse. Christ, then, is the necessary point of reference. This means that Christian faith is constituted of that same personal total self-giving to God which Jesus lived and commanded (love God). Similarly, because the remembered life of Christ which is central was the servant life, Christian faith is a dynamic which expresses itself in concrete loving concern for others (love neighbor). True faith inevitably impels works of love because the servant Christ's own life was a work of love. And *Agape's* continuing source, again as was the case with Jesus, is the joy of accepting God's love for one's self.

St. Paul, then, does not cast works in a secondary role; instead, he sets them in a new perspective. Formerly he had himself endeavored to win God's good will by scrupulously "doing the law" in all its detail. As a Christian, he could see why he had been utterly miserable in that earlier attempt. For one thing, to center one's existence upon law is actually to yield to sin, the chief sin of all—hubris—which assumes man's self-sufficiency and bargains with God as an equal. However, the Christian way of unreserved submission to the divine sovereignty by no means eliminates works. On the contrary, it underlines their imperative and their inevitability, because to love God is to obey his will: "You shall love your neighbor." Paul's view here is close to that which we attributed to the Situation Ethic in the first chapter. It stands midway between legalism on the one hand and license allowing self-gratification on the other. The principle of law for the Christian is invalid; but the freedom which faith bestows is a freedom with responsibility. The Christian is liberated from slavery to the law in order that in Christ he may be free to serve others.

The misunderstanding which St. Paul had to face in his day is no mere antiquarian curiosity. It is for this reason that we have considered his doctrine of faith at such length. The erroneous conclusion that works are peripheral has, in many different guises, plagued the Christian church and, as we hinted earlier, has inhibited her witness throughout history, and even in our own time. Few would subscribe to such an extreme position as "one need but have faith and let the world go by." And yet this view has been a constant tendency and temptation that has subtly deterred many from full commitment to be, like Christ, servants at every time and in every place. Moreover, it functions as one of those hidden assumptions that abet the conviction that the church exists above all else to provide an island of solace and shelter from life's hard realities. This in turn, buttressed by the one-sided assertion that Christianity is solely a "spiritual" matter, has contributed to the false dichotomy, "religious versus secular," which has so often been used to inhibit Christian involvement in world affairs.

All of this, however, is sharply challenged by the biblical witness. Faith *and* works—never did St. Paul envisage or counsel that kind of freedom which centers upon self and cares little about the needs of others. The Christ of the New Testament (and of the church) was the servant of God *and* of man. And it is not self-love, but Christ's servant love, a love which denies such divisive categories as faith versus works, religious versus secular, or sacred versus profane, to which the Situation Ethic points as the ultimate criterion, as it is the ultimate power, for all human action. The popular slogan, "nothing matters but love," understood correctly is a stirring challenge to the church and to individuals to re-discover the Christian gospel and to renew their reason for being through genuine concern in action for God's world. "What then?" St. Paul asks, "Are we to sin because we are not under law but under grace? By no means!" (Rom. 6:15). To be under grace is to be dominated by God's love. And *Agape* not only re-creates one's self, but also impels one to labor for the renewal of others.

St. Paul's pastoral concern for the daily lives of his converts is apparent on almost every page of his letters. Nothing, however, more clearly demonstrates the intensity and depth of his conviction concerning the inseparability of faith and *Agape* than does what he has to say about the two chief Christian sacraments, Baptism and the Eucharist. The passages in which he discusses these sacred rites are of special importance for the history of sacramental theology. Less frequently, however, and regrettably so, has full weight been given to the fact that the Apostle's chief references to both were prompted by concern for the proper exercise of Christian love. He insisted that Baptism and the Eucharist alike mediate an inherent ethical imperative that must be recognized and acted upon if right theology or proper liturgy are to be more than mere irrelevancies.

His most important reference to Baptism occurs in Romans 6 where he speaks of the immersion into the baptismal water as a dying and rising with Christ on the part of each convert: "Do you not know that all of us who have been baptized into Christ Jesus were baptized into his death? We were buried therefore with him by baptism into death, so that as Christ was raised from the dead by the glory of the Father, we too might walk in newness of life" (Rom. 6:3, 4). These words predicate two fundamentals of primitive Christian faith which are stressed repeatedly throughout the New Testament. The first is the conviction that Christ's death has, for those of faith, effected divine forgiveness for all past sin. It is this which is recalled by the phrase "baptized into his death."

Secondly, these verses presuppose the belief that Christ's resurrection assures the baptized Christian that he too will rise at the last day. As is apparent from numerous biblical texts, the "death-resurrection" pattern of Christ's existence has as its counterpart the "death-resurrection" of those who live in Christ. St. Paul himself, immediately following these two verses, affirms that "we shall certainly be united with him in a resurrection like his" (Rom. 6:5; cf. 1 Thess. 4:13–18, 1 Cor. 15).

Returning now to verses 3 and 4, it is clear that the Apostle is employing this traditional "death-resurrection" pattern, but that he has modified it. The statement, "as Christ was raised from the dead by the glory of the Father" would have as its natural complement something like, "we too might rise at the last day." Instead, Paul writes, *we too might walk in newness of life.* This substitution which refers to life here and now gives us the clue we need for understanding why Paul discusses Baptism at this point in his letter, and what it means to him.

In this connection it is important to note the Apostle's introduction in verses 1 and 2. Here he is referring to that antinomian misinterpretation of his position regarding faith against which he spoke so sarcastically in Romans 3:5–8. To the claim that sin matters little because God is so forgiving, he now indignantly replies, "By no means!" He then proceeds, in verses 3 and 4, against this background of deep concern for sin, to remind his readers that their Baptism refutes such preposterous nonsense. In Baptism they have died to the past and risen to a new beginning. Obviously, he in effect says, Christians are committed to the Christ life with all that this involves in terms of sinlessness and love. And yet Paul is not content with this generality, and he has chosen his words in verse 4 with care. The verb "walk" is of particular importance. Predominantly in the New Testament, and throughout St. Paul's letters, the original Greek word has an ethical cast signifying the manner of one's daily life as measured by Christian standards of behavior. Thus the Apostle makes it perfectly clear that the new beginning, the new life, is one that has the deepest ethical significance.

St. Paul's purpose, then, is clear. He seeks to refute those who suggest that Christian faith and everyday living have little to do with each other. He states, first, that an individual's emergence out of the baptismal water, even though it has significance for a more remote future (resurrection at the last day), is a here-and-now rising with Christ. Secondly, he insists that this new present "risen" life is one of strenuous ethical commitment. In Baptism the Christian dies to his former life in bondage to sin; his past is no more. Beyond this, however, he is incorporated into the servant Christ's own self-denying and self-giving life. And again, there is one word which sums up all that the day by day Christ-Christian life is and does: *Agape*. We have not attempted in these brief paragraphs to delineate all that Baptism meant to St. Paul and the early church, but this at least is clear: Baptism commits one irrevocably to that love for others which is the essence of the servant Christ's life.

The principle of *Agape* is no less integral to St. Paul's total understanding of the early Christian Eucharist. It is noteworthy that both of his overt references to this rite occur in a letter to Christians who, to his firsthand knowledge and sorrow, were "unloving," split with factionalism, and notably lacking in ability to apply their new faith to practical circumstances. In both instances, it was a pastoral concern about the lack of *Agape* which led the Apostle to speak of the Eucharist. As we shall see, he viewed the breaking of bread as a dramatic and effectual representation of Christ's love for the world and of the participating Christian's love for others.

His most lengthy comment occurs in 1 Corinthians 11:17–34. The immediate background for this passage was the early custom of meeting together in a believer's home for meals which were provided not only for community fellowship, but also as a practical good work for the poorer members. It was during such meals that a primitive form of the Eucharist was frequently celebrated. At a given moment, that is, bread would be broken and a cup of wine blessed as a specific and vivid recalling of Christ's last meal with the disciples on the eve of his death. This description will have a familiar ring to any reader who has been privileged to take part in the "house Eucharists" which have become so meaningful for many families in recent years.

The difficulty that had arisen in Corinth is plainly stated: "For in eating, each one goes ahead with his own meal, and one is hungry and another is drunk. What! Do you not have houses to eat and drink in? Or do you despise the church of God and humiliate those who have nothing?" (vss. 21, 22). Those who arrived early began to eat and drink, and became sated. Those who came late found little or nothing left, and for impoverished Christians, who benefited in a very material way from such meals, this was no small matter. The Apostle's comment is blunt: "What shall I say to you? Shall I commend you in this? No, I will not" (vs. 22).

Paul was upset, of course, because that which was intended as an effectual expression of community oneness and mutual concern had become an occasion for individual greed and selfishness. Over and beyond this, the Corinthians' selfishness underscored their serious misunderstanding of the fundamental principle that genuine faith is active in love. This is made clear by that which follows in verses 23–30 where St. Paul speaks of that specific Eucharistic action which was a part of the fellowship meal, and actually employs words that were used by some early Christian communities as a part of the Eucharistic rite: "the Lord Jesus on the night when he was betrayed took bread, and when he had given thanks, he broke it, and said, 'This is my body which is broken *for you.*

Do this in remembrance of me.' In the same way also the cup, after supper, saying, 'This cup is the new covenant *in my blood*. Do this, as often as you drink it, *in remembrance of me'* " (vss. 23–25).

Why does Paul quote this liturgical fragment? The italicized phrases point to the answer. The words recall in a manner both poignant and dramatic the servanthood of Christ. Used at each Eucharist, they reminded the participants (and should have reminded the Corinthians) that Jesus' breaking and blessing on the last night of his life had been (as we noted in Chapter II) a dramatic anticipatory offering of himself out of love on the cross—a self-offering in which each of those present at that final meal shared, and from which each benefited. And when, in verse 26, St. Paul goes on to say, "For as often as you eat this bread and drink the cup, *you proclaim the Lord's death* until he comes," he is reminding his readers that to "make Eucharist" is on every occasion to renew one's acceptance of that servant love with all that it means, its demand no less than its joy.

For Paul, then, the church's breaking of bread was intimately related to the love-in-action which *Agape* is, and which the life and death of Jesus so vividly made real. More than this, each celebration of the Eucharist was seen as a remembrance and a contemporary renewing of Christ's own enabling love and as a renewing, as well, of that "neighbor love" which is inherent to the life in Christ. This is confirmed by the Apostle's other important Eucharistic reference which occurs in 1 Corinthians 10:16, 17: "The cup of blessing which we bless, is it not a participation in the blood of Christ? The bread which we break, is it not a participation in the body of Christ? Because there is one loaf, we who are many are one body, for we all partake of the same loaf."

In Chapter 10 as a whole the Apostle's over-all concern is that same problem of meat sacrificed to idols which we discussed previously. His immediate purpose in referring to the

Eucharist at this point is to underline the oneness of Christians with Christ and with one another as a unity which must
be jealously guarded against any compromise, either real or
seeming. Of particular interest to us, however, is what these
words reveal, almost incidentally, about the meaning that the
Eucharist had for many early Christians. There is, St. Paul
affirms, one Christ, "one loaf," and "one body" which is the
church consisting of many members; and in the breaking and
sharing of the bread these individual members apprehend
anew their oneness with the Christ who died for them *and*
their oneness with all those others for whom he similarly gave
his life. The breaking of bread, moreover, actually effects
this oneness: "we who are many are one body, [*because*] we
all partake of the same loaf." And because the one Christ who
is encountered in the sharing of the one loaf is the servant
Christ whose love for God and man is the heart beat of
the Christian life, it follows that the Eucharistic rite was
(and is) at one and the same moment the source and expression par excellence of Jesus' own injunction "love God, love
neighbor."

That this was indeed St. Paul's understanding, and the
primary reason for his concern about the Corinthians' meal
fellowship, is confirmed by his shock and his sharp remarks
in Chapter 11. He says, in effect: Christ died for all, including,
specifically, those poor in your congregation who so desperately
need the loving concern of the more fortunate, and you are
celebrating the sacrament of Christ's love in an unloving
context of callous greed. In so doing you deny all that the
Eucharist is and is meant to be; because your blatant disregard
of those whom it is your vocation to love is an attack upon
the very fabric of the Christian community and its life as the
body of Christ. No, he sadly remarks, "When you meet together, it is not the Lord's supper that you eat" (vs. 20). How
can it be? And he warns of judgment: "For any one who eats
and drinks without discerning the body"—without, that is,

loving concern for those persons who are Christ's body, the church—"eats and drinks judgment upon himself" (vs. 29).

"You shall love your neignbor!" St. Paul's biting comments upon the Corinthians' table fellowship make very plain indeed the pre-eminence of *Agape* in his understanding of what the Christian life is and does. We have seen, as well, that for him *Agape* and the Lord's Supper are indissolubly linked together. It was Christ's servant love which first gave the Eucharist birth; that same love for all time lies at its center. And unless, however imperfectly, love is at the core of one's daily life, protestations of right faith including, St. Paul would say, the breaking of bread and the blessing of the cup, can bring only condemnation. The life in Christ is impelled and informed by love, and must express love for all. Anything less is to make of the Eucharist an empty legalism. One wonders if St. Paul, as he wrote, had in the back of his mind these stern words: "So if you are offering your gift at the altar, and there remember that your brother has something against you, leave your gift there before the altar and go; first be reconciled to your brother, and then come and offer your gift" (Mt. 5:23, 24).

Right knowledge, right theology, and right worship—these are good, and important. But unless they are informed by love, preserve the gospel of love, and impel and strengthen love's action, they become but alternate forms of a stifling legalism.

According to St. Paul, then, as it was for Christ, so it is for the Christian: Faith, and love-in-action for others, go hand in hand. At the same time, we have frequently seen that *Apape*'s demand summons the Christian to tasks which can be extremely difficult. Love often necessitates putting aside every vestige of self-interest; it requires persistence in one's efforts for another even when there is no satisfying response; hardest of all, it demands that the Christian care deeply for the unlovely. Its application requires objectivity, strict disci-

pline of both intellect and will, and not a little plain old
fashion stubbornness. It is not surprising, then, that the
Situation Ethic, which has this kind of love at its center,
offers neither simple solutions nor an easily followed road.
After all, its model (and the source of its strength) is not the
illusory gentle Jesus so often portrayed in Sunday School
leaflets, but the suffering servant of the cross.

St. Paul was fully aware of the difficulties. He believed that
to be baptized into Christ was to accept the demand to love
others as a daily and lifelong vocation. He also knew that no
man, by himself, can possibly measure up to such a task.
Nevertheless, he was confident that with the strength supplied
by God all things are possible; and he made a special effort
to win his converts to a realization of this. To this end he
repeatedly stressed the empowering role played by the Holy
Spirit in Christian lives. More specifically, the will and ability
to labor for others is not attainable by our own efforts. Ultimately, *Agape* is a gift of God's Holy Spirit.

There are many references to the Spirit in the New Testament. We must pause briefly to ask what St. Paul and early
Christians meant by this word. In the Old Testament the
phrase "Spirit of God" most frequently refers to powerful
divine activity. It is, for example, through his Spirit that God
creates, commands, governs, inspires, saves, and accomplishes
his manifold purposes with his world. So it was that Jesus
attributed his remarkable ability to heal not to himself, but
to the powerful Spirit of God at work through him: "But
if it is by the Spirit of God that I cast out demons, then
the kingdom of God has come upon you" (Mt. 12:28). Early
Christians, moreover, believed that they had been endowed
with that same Spirit from on high. This was their way of
saying that the new life in Christ, so wonderfully different
from what they had known before, was God's doing, God's
gift, the Spirit of God manifestly at work, recreating, upturning, inspiring, empowering. St. Paul sums it up this way:

"For by one Spirit we were all baptized into one body—Jews or Greeks, slaves or free—and all were made to drink of one Spirit" (1 Cor. 12:13).

The Spirit of God, then, was (and is) not something that one could see with the naked eye. Its effects, however, were evident, and often, according to the biblical records, manifested themselves in startling ways. Here one thinks of the varieties of individual "spiritual gifts," as St. Paul calls them, such as "the utterance of wisdom," "the utterance of knowledge," "gifts of healing," "the working of miracles," "prophecy," "various kinds of tongues," and "the interpretation of tongues" (1 Cor. 12:4–11, 27–31; Rom. 12:3–13). In gifts such as these, and in the air of almost palpable tension and excitement which characterized the early Christian assemblies and, most important of all, in the underlying new perspective, new courage, new joy, and new hope which dominated their lives, believers discerned something undeniably real—evidence of a very tangible nature of the continual presence of that Spirit which they had received at the time of their Baptism, a presence which made itself felt in many ways differing according to the individual and the occasion.

What, now, of *Agape*? St. Paul's answer is one of his most perceptive contributions to the treasury of Christian understanding. Love, he affirms, is the most important of all of the gifts of the one Spirit—the same Spirit, it is important to note, to which Jesus attributed the enabling power of his own demonstrably loving life. In such manner the Apostle, as pastor, speaks directly to the very practical question of how one can measure up to *Agape*'s demand. Do not be afraid, he reassures his readers. Those who accept Christ as Lord will have at their command that same power to love which dominated every moment of Jesus' own servant life. To be a Christian is to be in the Spirit, and herein lies one's ability to love others.

The priority of *Agape* among the gifts of the Spirit is

indicated repeatedly. In Galatians 5:22, for example, love heads the list: "But the fruit of the Spirit is love, joy, peace, patience, kindness, goodness, faithfulness, gentleness, self-control; against such there is no law." It is discussed briefly in the enumeration of gifts detailed in Romans 12:6–21: "Let love be genuine; hate what is evil, hold fast to what is good; love one another with brotherly affection; outdo one another in showing honor. Never flag in zeal, be aglow with the Spirit, serve the Lord" (vss. 9–11). It is singled out for special stress in Romans 13:8–10, a passage already commented upon at the beginning of this chapter. Yet again, in Colossians 3:12–14 love is the chief of those qualities that characterize the Christian life, the gift, moreover, that gives coherence to all else: "Put on then, as God's chosen ones, holy and beloved, compassion, kindness, lowliness, meekness, and patience, forbearing one another and, if one has a complaint against another, forgiving each other; as the Lord has forgiven you, so you also must forgive. And above all these put on love, which binds everything together in perfect harmony."

St. Paul's best known discussion of *Agape* appears in 1 Corinthians 13. In the preceding chapter he has spoken of the various manifestations of the Spirit at great length. Then, at the very end, and very pointedly, he states that he will now show his readers a "still more excellent way" (12:31). Immediately there follows in Chapter 13 the familiar paean to love which is hymned as that spiritual gift which has precedence over all others. Without love, all else is as nothing: "If I speak in the tongues of men and of angels, but have not love, I am a noisy gong or a clanging cymbal. And if I have prophetic powers, and understand all mysteries and all knowledge, and if I have all faith, so as to remove mountains, but have not love, I am nothing. If I give away all I have, and if I deliver my body to be burned, but have not love, I gain nothing" (13:1–3). Moreover, *Agape* is the one gift which is immutable and endures forever: "Love never ends; as for prophecy, it

will pass away; as for tongues, they will cease; as for knowledge, it will pass away" (vs. 8). The Apostle's final words in
this chapter are among the best known in the entire New
Testament: "So faith, hope, love abide, these three; but the
greatest of these is love" (vs. 13).

The importance of these final words, and of 1 Corinthians
13 in its entirety, can hardly be overestimated. No more than
did Jesus, of course, does St. Paul think in the perspective, or
employ the thought forms and the technical vocabulary ("situationism," "criterion," "absolute") of today's moral theologians. Nevertheless, in 1 Corinthians 13 he does speak in a
manner contiguous with our current idiom. There are, he
affirms, many important criteria for Christian action, and
many virtues that a Christian should cultivate. All, however,
must be motivated and undergirded by love. Furthermore, all
such "goods" are transitory, whereas "*Agape* never ends," is
unchanging, and is demanded and applicable in every conceivable circumstance. Immediately and inevitably one thinks
of today's Situation Ethic. It, too, insists that *Agape* is the one
enduring criterion for human relationships which never fails.
Obviously, there are other "goods" or actions or laws which
often, perhaps in most cases, effectively answer love's demand.
But these are always subject to challenge because, as history
itself demonstrates, that which is the most "loving" action in
one situation is not necessarily so in every circumstance. *Agape*
alone—the struggle to determine and effect the best good of
persons—as a golden thread that binds all together stands
immutable and sure, serving as a springboard for decision and
action in every age, in every culture, and for every individual.

What, specifically, does love demand in given instances?
Often the answers do not come easily, and there is disagreement. Some even may remain convinced that the very nature
of Christian love is such that it will always approve or inhibit
certain actions which, they would insist, are "derived" absolutes never to be contravened. Be this as it may, St. Paul's

words in 1 Corinthians 13 make it abundantly clear that love must be both the beginning and the end and the "in-between" for the Christian's every relationship and every activity. And with this today's New Morality is in complete agreement.

With the strength that God supplies, then, self-giving love for others, no matter how difficult, is always possible. Right faith not only demands love, but immediately proves itself as God's power to that end. Aware of all this, Paul constantly exhorts his converts to become in reality that which they already are in potential. "Through love," he urges, "be servants of one another. For the whole law is fulfilled in one word, 'You shall love your neighbor as yourself'" (Gal. 5:13, 14). And when, as happens so frequently, he speaks of living "in" or "by" or "according to the Spirit," he is reminding his readers that no longer, as in times past, are they dominated by that weakness which so plagues life "in the flesh." They now possess the strength which God himself supplies, enabling them to fulfill their baptismal promise to "walk in newness of life." "Walk by the Spirit," he exhorts, "and do not gratify the desires of the flesh. For the desires of the flesh are against the Spirit, and the desires of the Spirit are against the flesh; for these are opposed to each other, to prevent you from doing what you would" (Gal. 5:16, 17). For Paul, that is, the Spirit is no mere figure of speech, but a constant and powerful warrior ally at work in the service of *Agape* in the Christian's daily life: "For though we live in the world we are not carrying on a worldly war, for the weapons of our warfare are not worldly but have divine power to destroy strongholds" (2 Cor. 10:3, 4). There is nothing soft or sentimental about *Agape*. It is an indomitable protagonist which is never discouraged and never ceases.

The Christian, then, lives in the Spirit, and through the Spirit is emboldened and strengthened for service. What now of the fact that St. Paul, with equal frequency, speaks of

Christian existence as life "in Christ"? These texts are typical
of many: "So we, though many, are one body in Christ"; "for
you are all one in Christ Jesus"; "There is therefore now
no condemnation for those who are in Christ Jesus" (Rom.
12:5; Gal. 3:28; Rom. 8:1; cf. Gal. 5:6). Students of the
Apostle's letters frequently point out that the phrases "in
the Spirit" and "in Christ" are closely related—two alternative
ways, each with its own nuance, of describing one and the
same Christian existence. To inquire into the "how" and
"why" of this relationship further underlines Paul's practical
concern for the Christian ethical task.

St. Paul was apparently the first to use the expression "in
Christ," and its meaning owes much to his own deep religious
experience. Most important, for our purposes, is what this
brief phrase has to say about the nature of the Christian life.
As life "in Christ," the Christian experience at its deepest is
not, and never has been, simply a matter of intellectual assent
to a creed or to theological propositions, nor a subscription to
a code of rules. For the Christ of the church and of the world
is the person Jesus of Palestine whom death could not hold
and whom faith discerns as victoriously present and at work
wherever men may seek him. Hence the Christian life is a
relationship of person to person, with all that this means in
terms of inspiration, guidance, support, condemnation, for-
giveness, and love, between the believer and the Christ who
lives and reigns from the cross of love, a relationship so intimate and moving that many have employed the term "mys-
tical" in their attempts to describe it.

What now is the significance of St. Paul's insistence that
the Christian lives not only "in Christ," but simultaneously
"in the Spirit"? Although each phrase, as we noted, has its
own stress and special association, Paul uses the two as virtual
equivalents. It seems highly probable that he is making a
special point—that the undergirding force of the Christian
life (the Spirit) which demands, motivates, and impels, is not

some mechanical and abstract power, but the dynamic love of a person, Jesus Christ. Conversely, because to be "in Christ" is to be "in the Spirit," Paul is affirming that the personal union between the believer and his Lord, for all its intimacy and depth, is never static, never simply an I–Thou relationship selfishly existing for its own sake. On the contrary, because the Spirit manifests itself first and foremost as the demand and power to love others, union with Christ is dynamic and extrovert; it immediately drives one out into the world as servant of that world. Always, that is, involvement with Christ means simultaneous involvement with people in a relationship of love.

St. Paul's concept of personal union with Christ has rightly been regarded as one of his most significant insights into the nature of the Christian life. Too often in the past, however, the tendency has been to interpret this reality solely in individualistic and pietistic terms, and as something purely "spiritual" in the most circumscribed sense of that word. Seen in proper context, however, it is clear that the intimate union of which Paul speaks is activist through and through. As the close and purposeful relationship between the phrases "in Christ" and "in the Spirit" makes plain, the Apostle's concern was by no means simply other-worldly. Just as faith and love are inseparably one, so "in-Christness" has an inescapable ethical dimension. The essence of the Christian life is not withdrawal into a private shell, but a drive that thrusts outward. Relationship with Christ cannot be hugged to one's self and used as an antidote against reality and involvement. On the contrary, life in Christ sharpens one's awareness of the world's need, opens the heart, and moves into action. In short, to know the love of Christ is to love *all* those for whom he gave his life.

The preceding pages have made clear the profundity of St.

Paul's personal religious life. Underscoring the depth of his Christianity, and equally important for understanding his concept of *Agape,* is the strenuousness of his own commitment as an envoy of Christ throughout the Mediterranean world. Love for God and love for others constitute one whole. The Apostle understood this well.

At the center of his life was Christ, and Paul's perceptiveness regarding the nature of the Christ life. He had fastened upon Jesus' servanthood as the key, and knew that it was this same Christ-love that had overwhelmed him and continued to sustain his new life: "I live by faith in the Son of God, who loved me and gave himself for me" (Gal. 2:20). This same irresistible love, moreover, he knew to be the pivotal reality in Christ's relationship with all believers: "For you know the grace of our Lord Jesus Christ, that though he was rich, yet for your sake he became poor, so that by his poverty you might become rich" (2 Cor. 8:9).

There was more, however. This Christ-love proved to be so unique in the experience of those who had been seized by it that St. Paul, and Christians generally, found themselves compelled to see therein, as the only possible explanation, God's own love now revealed with a clarity and a power hitherto unknown: "But *God* shows his love for us in that while we were yet sinners Christ died for us"; "But *God*, who is rich in mercy, out of the great love with which he loved us . . . made us alive together with Christ . . ." (Rom. 5:8, Eph. 2:4,5). Also important in this connection is Romans 5:5 which all but equates that gift of the Spirit which is love's enabling power with God's own love: "because *God's* love has been poured into our hearts through the Holy Spirit which has been given to us." In short, continuing Christian experience was basically identical with that of those who had known Jesus at the very beginning and found themselves compelled to shout, "God has visited his people!" (Lk. 7:16). Then, and

now, St. Paul would say, the servant Christ life was and remains powerful to communicate that divine reality of love
which was its root and its message.

It was, then, Christ who made the difference. And there is
no clearer indication of what that difference was, or of its implications for daily living, than the words penned by the
Apostle after years of reflection upon what had happened
at the time of his conversion: "[God] called me through his
grace, was pleased to reveal his Son to me" (Gal. 1:15, 16).
His new life, that is, was simply and solely the gift of God's
love. And from that point on he knew himself to be a man
"under grace": "But by the grace of God I am what I am"
(1 Cor. 15:10). Significantly, however, he does not stop here.
In the same verse he adds, "and [God's] grace toward me was
not in vain. On the contrary, I worked harder than any of
them." Here he refers to his labor as an apostle; and noteworthy here is Paul's recognition that his work as a Christian
was an inevitable result of the grace received. God's gift, that
is, was not something to be hugged to himself; it had to be
shared.

These words, reflecting St. Paul's experience, call to mind
the basic pattern of Jesus' earthly ministry. His obedience to
the command to love neighbor had been more than a simple
accession to a divine fiat. For him, also, the ultimate source
had been God's grace. To surrender self to God's love is to
long above all else to do his will. Effective love for others,
then, springs not from fearful obedience to a command, but
from one's own free choice. Such, manifestly, was St. Paul's
own apprehension, and the pattern of his new Christian life.
Clearly, it was the servant Christ who had overwhelmed him
on the Damascus Road; and it was because of Christ's own
servanthood that he and all Christians had attained their
new vision of God as one who is deeply gracious.

There was, however, another factor which contributed to
the urgency of Paul's self-giving. He knew that the servant

love of Christ reveals and mediates the love of God himself. He also discerned—although this is more implicit than explicit in his letters—that Christ's love and God's love are one and the same. The significance of this is clear: The known love of Jesus for others is no mere model for human conduct, nor is it simply a superior virtue to be emulated as far as possible; rather, Christ-love is an imperative for the human situation because it is grounded in the very nature of the Divine Being. St. Paul never comes out and says it in so many words, but it lies just beneath the surface of all that he writes about *Agape*—that in Christ man discerns not only *God's way for* his world, but equally *God's own way with* his world. The author of 1 John, as we shall see, states it explicitly: "for God is love" (4:8).

Ultimately, then, the command to love others derives from the very being of God himself. To recognize this is to be struck with special force by the urgency which underlies today's Situation Ethic. Its concern centers upon that which, according to the gospels and St. Paul, is the very ground root of all existence. Indeed, the Christian New Morality is a serious ethical position with profound implications.

Finally, we turn to St. Paul's actual life as an apostle. He was perhaps the greatest missionary that the church has ever had, and it is not difficult to understand why. The joy of knowing God's love, standing in such sharp contrast to the frustrations of trying to lift himself up by his own bootstraps ("doing the law"), drove him outward and onward. About his past he wrote, "But whatever gain I had, I counted as loss for the sake of Christ. Indeed I count everything as loss because of the surpassing worth of knowing Christ Jesus my Lord" (Phil. 3:7, 8). And as far as the future was concerned, he could do no other than share the good news: "For necessity is laid upon me. Woe to me if I do not preach the gospel!" (1 Cor. 9:16). To belong to Christ was to know love's demand. Consequently, he devoted his new life of faith to the *work* of a missionary and apostle.

"Paul, a servant of Christ, called to be an apostle, set apart for the gospel of God" (Rom. 1:1). How did he understand this apostolic office? First of all, it was a commission that came from God, the result of a divine initiative and a divine call. That is, the life in Christ is never an end in itself. Always, to accept God's love is to accept God's demand. Nor was the fact that he had been called in any sense cause for boasting. It was an election not to status and privilege, but to service: "For what we preach is not ourselves, but Jesus Christ as Lord, with ourselves as your servants for Jesus' sake" (2 Cor. 4:5).

Apostleship, moreover, is love-in-action, a labor which mediates the very material benefits of God's own loving concern for people: "The signs of a true apostle were performed among you in all patience, with signs and wonders and mighty works" (2 Cor. 12:12). Still more, apostleship must surrender personal preferences and, not least, effective concern for others often inhibits the full exercise of that freedom which is God's gift to the man in Christ: "For though I am free from all men, I have made myself a slave to all, that I might win the more. To the Jews I became as a Jew, in order to win Jews; to those under the law I became as one under the law . . . that I might win those under the law. To those outside the law I became as one outside the law . . . that I might win those outside the law. To the weak I became weak, that I might win the weak. I have become all things to all men, that I might by all means save some" (1 Cor. 9:19–22). Finally, apostleship means hardship; for love is often repelled: "To the present hour we hunger and thirst, we are ill-clad and buffeted and homeless, and we labor, working with our own hands. When reviled, we bless; when persecuted, we endure; when slandered, we try to conciliate; we have become, and are now, as the refuse of the world, the offscouring of all things" (1 Cor. 4:11–13).

According to St. Luke, Jesus said, "I must preach the good news of the kingdom of God to the other cities also; for *I was sent* for this purpose" (Lk. 4:43). He in turn commissioned others: "As thou didst send me into the world, so have *I sent them* into the world" (Jn. 17:18). Moreover, an apostle is *"one sent"*; this is the root meaning of the underlying Greek word. And the foundation stone of apostleship (as of every Christian life) is Christ who was *sent* forth into the world, and that life in Christ which has the humility to be *sent* and to be spent. A true apostle will visibly manifest that total acceptance of God's love which constitutes the powerful outward thrust of *Agape* toward all. St. Paul would be the first to say that where deep and effective concern for all men is lacking, the apostolic office has become a travesty of God's intent. And his own apostolic life witnessed to that same servant love which is so fundamental to the contemporary Situation Ethic.

IV

Saint John: God Is Love

The New Testament's concept of *Agape* has a depth and a comprehensiveness that far exceed what appears at a first casual reading. This, by itself, forcefully suggests that the Christian New Morality, which has the same love as its fundamental principle, is a phenomenon more informed and more compelling than is apparent from its popularized presentations. St. John, to whose writings we now turn, reinforces this judgment. For him, too, Christian love is of the highest importance. Although we have already quoted him upon occasion, his gospel and epistles deserve special attention for many reasons.

St. John, for one thing, stresses *Agape* more than any other New Testament writer, and he alone considers its many ramifications with such systematic and deliberate care. Furthermore, he occupies a position of particular pre-eminence among early Christian leaders as an intellectual and as a theologian. His theological evaluation of Christ, for example, has a profundity which many would contend is unequaled by that of any other biblical author. And not least in importance is St.

John's mature and balanced spirituality. He has meditated at great length upon the Christian revelation and has thoroughly tested its meaning at the practical level of everyday living.

The importance of these particular characteristics will become clearer as we look at John's writings in detail, but their presence and interaction in a single individual are so striking that they demand one anticipatory comment: This great Christian offers a sharp contradiction to that divisive compartmentalization of theology, spirituality, and ethics that so often leads to preference for one and lack of interest in, and so neglect of, another. Not only does St. John insist that the Christian's ethical concern and conduct, in order to be fully effective, must be thoroughly grounded in theology and personal religious experience, but also he holds, and is himself his own best example, that a "high" Christology has as its inevitable accompaniment a "high" ethic, and that genuine spirituality and ethical awareness and commitment in action are indissolubly related. His careful analysis of *Agape* brings both parts of Jesus' summary command into sharp focus and, in so doing, enhances the Situation Ethic's claim that it is an expression of the mind of Christ.

Turning now to St. John's text, such representative passages as these show the centrality of love in his thinking: "This is my commandment, that you love one another as I have loved you"; "For this is the message which you have heard from the beginning, that we should love one another"; "He who does not love does not know God; for God is love" (Jn. 15:12; 1 Jn. 3:11, 4:8; cf. Jn. 13:34, 2 Jn. 5). John explicitly verbalizes the command to love far more than do the other Evangelists or St. Paul. It is significant, also, that while he frequently refers in general terms to the "commandments," either of God or of Christ, as an important part of the Christian life, the only one of these which he chooses to detail with any regularity in either the gospel or the epistles is love. So much does he dwell upon *Agape* in 1 John that this letter has often been called "The Epistle of Love." There is no question, as will become increasingly apparent, but that the Situation Ethic can justifiably add the Johannine Literature to its list of confirmatory biblical witnesses to the overwhelming importance of *Agape*.

The texts cited above refer to love for other people. Equally important, as St. John knew, is love for God. Like St. Paul, he avows that one can neither recognize nor answer *Agape*'s demands if he relies solely upon human resources. It is with this in mind that John records the famous analogy of the vine (Jn. 15:1–11). "I am the vine, you are the branches" (vs. 5). The branches are an integral part of the vine; they are supported by it and utterly dependent upon it for life and strength and fruitfulness: "He who abides in me, and I in him, he it is that bears much fruit, for apart from me you can do nothing" (vs. 5). The warning in these words is self-explanatory. To be severed from the vine is to die; relationship with Christ is a "must." Reliance upon the life which is supplied by God through Christ is a prerequisite for everything else. "You shall love the Lord your God."

"You shall love your neighbor"—the analogy of the vine speaks to this also, and with equal forcefulness. It is not just chance that the very first point which is made after the introductory words of verse 1 comprises the warning: "Every branch of mine that bears no fruit, [God] takes away, and every branch that does bear fruit he prunes that it may bear more fruit" (vs. 2). Furthermore, verses 4 and 5, even as they emphasize the necessity for dependence upon Christ, make it clear that this relationship has the bearing of fruit as one of its primary ends. The words speak for themselves. Union with Christ is essential—but always for a purpose which lies beyond the personal joy which it brings. And precisely what purpose is made clear in verses 12 and 13: "This is my commandment, that you love one another as I have loved you. Greater love has no man than this, that a man lay down his

life for his friends." To abide in Christ's love (vs. 9) is to love
one's neighbor.

Like others before him, then, but with special care and
emphasis, John speaks to the necessary balance of the Christian life. He is another who got the point: Jesus lived totally
for others, and his servant love took both its origin and its
strength from complete surrender of self to God. St. Paul, as
we observed, adheres to the same pattern when he insists that
right faith proves itself through works of love, or when he
affirms that to be in Christ is at the same moment to be in the
Spirit which empowers one to love. So it is that the Johannine
Christ says, "Apart from me you can do nothing" and, in the
same breath, "Love one another" (Jn. 15:5, 12).

The sharp explicitness of St. John's equal stress upon both
parts of Jesus' summary injunction is especially appropriate to
the circumstances in which the Christian church finds herself
today. It offers both encouragement and warning. The church,
although not without controversy and pain, is presently wres-
tling with a more acute awareness of responsibility, which is
urging her to prophetic and participating engagement with
the great social issues of contemporary life. In this connection,
it may be anticipated, situationists will play an increasing
role; because the emphasis upon self-giving love, which characterizes this ethical stance, clearly stirs the conscience to a
more wholehearted response to human need wherever it
exists. St. John, we may be certain, would be the first to
approve.

At the same time he would utter a warning: Activism which
has no roots is in danger of self-destruction. It is important to
remember here that both he and St. Paul penned their exhor-
tations about neighbor love in the context of vital Christian
communities whose foundation stone was the worship of God
in Christ. It was as themselves participating members that
both knew the vocation and the strength and the joy of self-
giving love, which obedience to the servant Christ brings. It

is inconceivable that either one, apart from this nourishing context, could have known and passed on to succeeding generations the richness of life in Christ. And both, we may be sure, would counsel against that kind of impatience which leads people simply to be up and doing without sufficient recognition and reflection as to the "why" and "how" of their activity.

This is not a simplistic plea on behalf of traditional pietism in traditional surroundings. What Paul and John have to say goes deeper. Both knew that the kind of tough, never ceasing, self-denying love of which the New Testament speaks is possible only if one recognizes and relies upon that which transcends himself. How, apart from Christ, they would ask, can one know what *Agape* really is? And how, except in Christ, can *Agape* find its strength? And it is significant (and a hopeful sign) that so many of those who today advocate the New Morality are to be found still within the church, even though they find themselves compelled to be sharply critical of much that constitutes formal Christianity. It is their experience that, despite the manifest faults of the church and her members, it is here in the corporateness of the worshiping community that they are most vividly aware of the continuing presence and life-giving power of the servant Christ.

St. John's admonitions with respect to mere activism are matched by equally stern warnings against that kind of ingrown piety which has no effective concern for others' needs. The long history of Christianity shows that man's fundamental problem—idolization of self—is no less rampant when it comes to "religion" than it is anywhere else. Many, perhaps most, yield to the subtle temptation to use the church's daily round as a kind of magical charm which guarantees *my* joy, *my* salvation. John was aware of this danger, as was Jesus himself: "For whoever would save his life will lose it; and whoever loses his life for my sake and the gospel's will save it" (Mk. 8:35). The gospel that Jesus proclaimed was the very opposite of *self*-concern. Only through self-*giving* is salvation possible. St. John goes out of his way to combat any and all manifestations of an introverted Christianity. For him, any activity or attitude which inhibits an effective sense of responsibility for others is completely contrary to the Christ life.

On this point he is especially insistent. Did he perhaps consider this problem more crucial even than rootless activism? There is a whole series of texts that sting with the explicit warning that a faith that is not fruitful is simply no faith at all. He writes, for example, "Little children, let us not love in word or speech but in deed and in truth. By this we shall know that we are of the truth, and reassure our hearts before him" (1 Jn. 3:18, 19). He comments elsewhere: "If we claim to be sharing in his life while we walk in the dark"—the reference is to the unloving life—"our words and our lives are a lie" (1 Jn. 1:6, NEB). Christian faith, that is, always expresses itself through acts of love. The equation between right faith and *Agape* is especially apparent in such sayings as these: "If"—the crucial word—"*If* you keep my commandments, you will abide in my love"; "*If* you love me, you will keep my commandments" (Jn. 15:10, 14:15).

Such statements as these are unmistakably clear. In a manner and with an emphasis unmatched by any other New Testament writer, John seizes upon *Agape* as absolutely essential and boldly equates it with the genuineness of one's Christianity. This is an accent which dovetails with his suggestion, in other connections, that in the final analysis Christianity authenticates itself in its doing. The Johannine Christ, for example, says, "if any man's will is to do [God's] will, he shall know whether the teaching is from God or whether I am speaking on my own authority" (Jn. 7:17). Nothing, however, more decisively underlines this important experiential aspect of Christian faith than St. John's insistence that man's knowledge of God and Christ is inseparably linked with the "doing" of *Agape*. He states categorically, "He who does not love does not know God; for God is love" (1 Jn. 4:8). "No man has ever seen God," he adds a few lines below, but "if we love one another, God abides in us and his love is perfected in us" (1 Jn. 4:12). Most pointed of all is 1 John 4:20: "If any one says, 'I love God,' and hates his brother, he is a liar; for he who does not love his brother whom he has seen, cannot love God whom he has not seen."

Is St. John saying in these texts that the *only* way to see God is to look into the faces of other people and answer their needs? We should not, perhaps, press him on the matter; but he comes close to this point. At the very least he would say this: In man's often painful response of love to the joys and sorrows and needs of others there is always present that reality of God which Christ brought and which Christ is. This is to suggest, as well, a way of renewal for many to whom God now seems remote; for John's assurance is no less than this—that in the self-giving (and receiving) which is the essence of *Agape*, humanity finds its truest and surest intimation with respect to the Deity for whom it so restlessly and relentlessly searches. To affirm that "God is love" does not exhaust man's knowledge about his Creator; but it is to be reassured that where love is, there indeed is God himself. These words from the famous Parable of the Last Judgment are directly to the point: "Then the righteous will answer him, 'Lord, when did we see thee hungry and feed thee, or thirsty and give thee drink? And when did we see thee a stranger and welcome thee, or naked and clothe thee? And when did we see thee sick or in prison and visit thee?' And the King will answer them, 'Truly, I say to you, as you did it to one of the least of these my brethren, you did it to me' " (Mt. 25:37–40).

Without love for others, then, love for God is an utter impossibility. Is there, however, a certain contradictory element in John's thinking? At one moment, as in the analogy of the vine, he strongly affirms that the life in Christ is the foundation upon which all else must be constructed. At other times, as the immediately preceding paragraphs have made clear, he comes at least very close to saying that neighbor love is where one must begin, and that it is this alone which makes possible a subsequent knowledge of God.

We have no record that St. John came to any conclusion which resolves this apparent contradiction. It may be that his ambivalence was purposeful. At any rate, his silence suggests that he would have regarded arguments pro and con about priority less than exciting. Like St. Paul, he knew that the Christ-Christian life is one seamless robe, and in its totality something so much greater than human comprehension can fathom that paradoxical modes of expression are inevitable. Neither love for God nor love for man can be "the real thing" if either is isolated from the other. On the one hand, John pictures the Christian as constantly on his knees, and yet, at the same moment, impatient to be up and doing out in the streets where there are wants and needs which he alone can fulfill. From the other perspective he sees the Christian as active with deeds of love, and yet, in the very midst of his busyness, and without stopping for a single moment, aware in the deep stillness of his inmost self of God's empowering presence in and through it all. And the one constant which permeates and unifies the whole is the living Christ himself who is waiting and present in every need, and able always to supply what is lacking—for one's own needs as well as for those of others.

The Christian commitment as set forth by St. John is awesome in its depth and in its demand. Both he and St. Paul insisted that the Christian life at its core is a personal relationship with Christ. And for both, although John explicates it more dramatically than does the Apostle, this meant that *Agape* is paramount, because *Agape* is Christ-love.

St. John, however, did not stop here. Jesus enjoined love,

and therefore those in Christ must love—well and good. Helpful, also, is the model of that servant love that Jesus himself offers. But John was convinced that full recognition of the nature, the meaning, the urgency, and the power of such love depended upon one's correct apprehension of Jesus' ultimate significance. For this reason he took special pains to relate his own understanding of *Agape* with his theological evaluation of Christ. As a consequence, and making explicit what is implicit in the gospel picture of Jesus and in the letters of St. Paul, John offers a theological rationale for *Agape* which for the Christian constitutes an inescapable imperative to spend one's self for others.

We must first as a necessary introduction look briefly at St. John's Christology. In common with St. Paul and with early Christians generally, John found that the impact of Jesus upon the lives of those who followed him defied and overflowed all merely human categories of explanation. Who, indeed, was he? The only answer which proved to be at all adequate cried out that he must have been in some unique manner the very manifestation of God himself. It was to explicate this deep conviction that John fastened upon the concept of Jesus as the divine Logos (Word) of God.

This affirmation employed and filled with a new Christian content a type of philosophical and religious thought that was widespread throughout the Mediterranean world of the day. We need not concern ourselves with the many complexities of such non-Christian Logos speculation; but common to all were these basic presuppositions: The Deity, however it is understood, defined, or described, is one who communicates with a universe that is his, and does so through the agency of his Word, which was understood variously, and often interchangeably, as God's command, or divine governing reason, or Deity's effective power. By this Word (Logos) God creates, rules, sustains, and brings to fulfillment his purposes for the world. In brief, Logos was a term expressing the totality of

God's relationship with the universe. Many, moreover, thought of the activity of the Logos as a kind of extension, often personified, of the Divine Being. As the root principle of all existence the Logos was regarded as the source of all life, and as the communicating Word intelligible to man it was viewed as the means of knowledge about God and of saving communion with him.

Jesus, St. John declared, is the visible manifestation of that divine Logos. It is to this that he refers in the very first words of his gospel: "In the beginning was the Word, and the Word was with God, and the Word was God. He was in the beginning with God; all things were made through him, and without him was not anything made that was made. In him was life, and the life was the light of men" (1:1–4). Then John goes on to make the explicit identification: "And the Word became flesh and dwelt among us, full of grace and truth; we have beheld his glory, glory as of the only Son from the Father" (vs. 14).

It was by this means that St. John affirmed the ultimate and universal significance of Jesus Christ. What had happened in Palestine under Pontius Pilate was no local phenomenon of passing interest to a mere handful. On the contrary, to know this Jesus is to perceive in its full reality that divine revealing and saving Word which lies at the heart of all creation. St. Paul came close to saying the same thing when he wrote of Christ: "He is the image of the invisible God . . . all things were created through him and for him. He is before all things, and in him all things hold together" (Col. 1:15–17). That is, Christ is all in all, the beginning, the end, and everything that intervenes. Around him the entire universe, as it were, revolves; from him who is the divine Word the universe takes its meaning. Clearly, both Paul and John, through words such as these, have strongly accented the central paradox, the scandal, of the Christian faith—that in Jesus of Nazareth, one who was in all things a creature of history limited by historical circumstances precisely like ourselves, are none the less to be found the answers to man's deepest questions about the nature and the why and the wherefore of God, of all creation, and of human life itself.

This concept of the Logos Christ has proved to be especially important in theological discussion and definition throughout Christian history, and underlines St. John's stature as a theologian. However, our immediate interest is the relationship between the Logos-Christ concept and *Agape*, and there is every indication that it was one of John's special concerns as well.

It is in connection with his gospel that one sees this relationship most clearly. In the opening words, as we noted, he explicitly affirms that Jesus is the visible expression of that divine Logos which has existed with God from eternity (1:1–14). Having established this as his "text," for the main body of his account he selects and employs suitable elements of the tradition with respect to Jesus in such a way as to illustrate the indicated thesis. That is, John chooses those particular activities, relationships, and sayings which he believes best reflect that underlying divine reality which Christians found in Jesus and which the Logos doctrine explicates. Yet not once, after the identification of Jesus with the Logos in the introductory verses of the first chapter, is the title used of him again. Instead, the principle word employed to characterize the Logos Christ's motivations and activities is *Agape*.

Immediately one asks if this happened simply by chance, or by design. Has John perhaps deliberately substituted *Agape* for Logos? And when we recall that the love which is stressed so much in his gospel was indeed the most distinctive feature of Jesus' earthly life, the answer seems clear. St. John has to all intents and purposes made a kind of rough equation between Logos and *Agape*. He is affirming that the servant love of Jesus, which had so powerfully affected the lives of his followers, was no less than the chief manifestation and activity of that divine Logos which is God's own mode of self-expression in relation to his universe.

That this is indeed John's message is confirmed by a closer look at certain key representative texts. In a pattern strikingly reminiscent of current non-Christian Logos speculation, these passages, as we shall see, point to *Agape* as the fundamental reality which, emanating from God, permeates the world of men. In other words, Jesus' servant love is not simply the self-giving of one kindly individual. Rather, his love is the effective revelation of a divine cosmic principle which lies at the center of all existence. John's understanding here can best be representd by a crude diagram in which love is depicted as a continuous line leading from God to Christ, from Christ to the individual Christian, and from the Christian on out through the world to others.

For example, the line originates with the assertion "God is love," a statement which in the simplest possible manner summarizes that deeper awareness about God's nature which Christ had brought (1 Jn. 4:8). That divine love, however, is "agapeic," self-giving love-in-action, because Christ is the object of God's love, and the gift of divine love to the world: "For God so loved the world, that he gave his only Son" (Jn. 3:16; cf. 1 Jn. 4:9). That is, as St. Paul made clear with his references to divine love and grace, *Agape* is the manner of God's own way with the world. The next step in the progression of John's thought avers that Jesus' own love for others is grounded in that same divine love: "As the Father has loved me, so have I loved you" (Jn. 15:9). That is, it was God's love which sent his Son; now God's love for the world is mediated through that Son. And finally, St. John points to the love for others, which is enjoined upon every Christian, as inseparably an expression and sharing of that same divine love which Christ brought: "A new commandment I give to you, that you love one another; even as I have loved you, that you also love one another" (Jn. 13:34; cf. 13:14–16, 15:12).

The line of our crude diagram is now complete: God's love, Christ's love, the Christian's love. And the parallelism between *Agape* as a universal principle, and the role of the Logos as a like cosmic principle in both its non-Christian and Christian forms is inescapable. The divine Word was viewed as the Deity's mode of self-expression. Issuing forth from God, it creates, sustains, and effects the divine will. Jesus Christ, St. John asserts, is that divine Logos visibly manifested in time and space, and in a manner (human as we are human) accessible to finite understanding. And the importance of John's equating of Logos and *Agape* is now fully apparent. He has seized upon and boldly proposed love—the kind of self-giving love which characterized the life of Jesus—to be an alternative way of understanding and defining that initiating and undergirding principle that, commencing with God himself, like a single golden strand determines and gives coherence and meaning to all.

St. John's contribution here is one of incalculable importance. He has sought to explain in his own way and out of his own knowledge and religious experience that absolutely basic premise of early Christianity which we have often noted— that to know Christ's love is somehow to be seized and re-created by the love of God himself. He has succeeded brilliantly. What, he asked, is the true significance of Jesus' servant love and of its incomparable power for good? It was (and is), he replied, the penetration of God himself into and throughout his creation. And again the deep meaning of the substitution of "love" for "Logos" in the main body of the gospel is clear. John is saying that everything which can be affirmed of Christ because he is the divine Word, can and must be affirmed of *Agape* as well. As the divine Logos, Christ reveals the essence of what God is—and this, John asserts, is love; God is love. As the Logos expressive of God's will, the servant Christ likewise reveals what man is meant to be—one whose life is dominated by *Agape*. In Christ the life-giving

Logos, man finds the ability and the will to be that true self—
and this is the power of *Agape*. In short (to paraphrase our
earlier description of the Logos Christ), St. John affirms: "Love
is all in all, the beginning, the end, and everything that intervenes. Around love the entire universe . . . revolves. From
love the universe takes its origin and its meaning." To aver,
as have many, that love is the ground of all being has strong
biblical attestation.

St. John's substitution of *Agape* for Logos underlines his
acumen as a theologian. More important, it supplies *Agape*
with a theological imperative of the gravest import: Love for
neighbor, as a demand and as a joy, is grounded in the very
nature and activity of the Divine Being. Thus, as we hinted
in the preceding chapter, John explicates what St. Paul intimates: Love-in-action is God's way for his world because it is
God's own way with his world. John's Christianity, we observed, is a rebuke to those who would separate theology,
ethics, and the spiritual life into isolated categories. His insistence upon *Agape* as the primary activity of the divine
Logos is a striking case in point. More than this, one suspects
that here was a theologian as concerned for relevance as any
activist of our own day. As evidence we need but point to the
potential which his particular exposition of Christian love
has for the apologetic and pastoral task. The key to this
potential is John's realistic willingness to start with man
where he is. In other words, he takes as his point of departure
love as known and experienced on the human plain, and
insists that here is the clue which leads one on to right understanding with respect to God and his Christ. John's repeated
emphasis upon the necessity of "doing" *Agape* if we would
know the truth that "God is love" illustrates well this "ad
hominem" approach. Typical here is a text that we cited
earlier: "He who does not love does not know God; for God
is love" (1 Jn. 4:8).

Of particular value for the apologist today is the correspondence between John's stress upon human experience and
what actually happened on the ground floor of Christian
origins, because it throws light upon the claim that Christianity is an historical religion. It all began, as we know, with the
appearance of a man—the Jesus of history—and the evident
response which his life called forth from people who were
essentially like ourselves. Pivotal was this man's love for
others and its known power (no less after his crucifixion than
before) to penetrate and to renew. It was this, ultimately,
which impelled the joyful refrain "God is love," *but*—and
John we may suspect was very much aware of this—the new
Christian vision of Deity was occasioned by a human Jesus
whose human love was humanly expressed and humanly experienced. Christianity, that is, has its beginning not in the
vague never-never land of a magical kind of supernaturalism
but in the stuff of history as we ourselves live it, and know it
to be. This fact also has a significant corollary. Precisely because its beginning and its focus are the human love of the
human Jesus, the love of which the New Testament speaks is
not so exaltedly "spiritual" or other-worldly that it is simply
incomprehensible to finite minds. Equally important is that
Christianity can never be set in opposition to or used to de-
nigrate that human experience of love which, according to
John, is inseparably related to it.

The apologetic and pastoral value of St. John's "theology
of *Agape*" is apparent in other connections as well. When, for
example, John posits the divine Logos and *Agape* as alternative ways of explaining the ultimate reality of all things, he
is affirming that man can and does know God in the warp
and woof of his daily human experience. The reason, of
course, is that self-giving for others (*Agape*) is something in
which every individual, however imperfectly, can and does
take part. The giving (and receiving) of love with its manifold
expressions is the most down to earth as well as the most

exalted of all human experiences. And it is precisely this love, which all to some degree can understand, which John insists is grounded in the very nature and activity of God himself. This is to say that all love correctly so called is "of God." Furthermore, John's thesis makes possible at least the beginning of an answer that will be meaningful when one is asked, "Who is God? What is he like? What does he do? Does he care?" In reply St. John would say, "Already, within your grasp, and as a part of your experience there exists that which you are seeking. God is love!"

Nor, John would continue, is this a matter simply of intellectual recognition and assent. Christ is the divine Logos. And that love of Christ, which man receives and shares with others, is divine love. This means that every moment of the give and take of human life that is informed by *Agape* is an encounter with God himself. Doubtless this is why, as we noted earlier, John so strongly insists that "doing" *Agape* is absolutely essential if one would know God. The wonder and mystery of the Divine Being are inexhaustible, and to say that "God is love" is but a beginning of understanding. But, John avers, it is a true beginning. He who would find the invisible God need not long for "miracles," nor for some kind of special revelation as "proofs" either that God exists or that he is active in one's life. In Christ, faith knows that in every instance of the giving and receiving of love one meets the unseen Deity face to face.

John's pastoral awareness also speaks encouragingly to the need felt by so many today for an anchor in the midst of change and bewilderment. This is the case because his virtual equating of Logos and love pinpoints *Agape*'s activity on the horizontal plain as a sure means of responding to the divine will. It is true that in this life we do not have final answers concerning God's purposes for the world and for ourselves. However, because love is of God, there is always the certainty, for all one's unanswered questions about ultimates, that there is a meaningful task to be done. Because love is God's way with his world and for his world, one knows that labor for others' good is always, as it were, life "with the grain." Faith in Christ as the revealer of God and of the power of his love brings with it the sure knowledge that the way of *Agape* is *the* way—one, moreover, which is ultimately irresistible in effecting good in and through every conceivable circumstance. All in all, St. John's perceptiveness points to a joy and a demand and a vocation that are specific, understandable, and realizable, one that makes for an existence with meaning and purpose even in the middle of doubts and uncertainties. To love is always right.

St. John, then, is a powerful and relevant apologist for the Christian faith. His reliance upon the idiom of human experience helped him to translate theological truth into understandable terms. John, we may suspect, had little interest in theology for its own sake. His concern, rather, was the day by day meaning of self-commitment to the Logos Christ in terms of the joy (of being loved) and the vocation (to love others) which such commitment brings. As a theologian, St. John, with a depth unmatched by any other New Testament writer, has explicated the ultimate and universal significance of Jesus Christ. At the same time, by translating the doctrinal affirmation of the Logos Christ into an impetus for daily living he has reaffirmed the basic biblical witness that Christianity is, in the final analysis, not a matter of intellectual propositions, but a way of life, the life in Christ.

What St. John has to say, moreover, "spotlights" the critical importance of today's Situation Ethic. When situationism avows that love is the key, its immediate interest is the very practical one of what is to be done, or not done, in concrete instances of decision-making and action. At the same time, its fundamental principle, *Agape,* goes far beyond matters of daily behavior. We can now recognize that the New Morality is urgently calling man to a recognition of his own true nature under God, and is affirming that man's personal future and the world's future depend upon accepting God's love for himself and sharing that love with others. For love is of God, and John has made it clear that the servant Christ is the incarnation of that divine love.

St. John, then, more explicitly and decisively than any other biblical writer points to love as the clue to human existence. *Agape*, he asserts, is "all in all." It is God's way with and for his world past, present, and future. This is John's special way of saying that "nothing matters but love." And for this, the ultimate reason is now clear—*with God himself nothing matters but love!* Clearly, the Christian New Morality which proclaims that same love as its fundamental "gospel" is no innovation. Rather, it is the familiar Christ of the New Testament and of traditional theology whom situationists seek to interpret and relate to a new age and to new circumstances.

It may seem as if the last few pages have carried us far from the Jesus of Nazareth with whom Christianity began. Actually, such is not the case. When St. John affirms that the demand and joy and pain of loving others is grounded in the very nature of God himself, he is neither speculating in thin air nor theologizing for its own sake. On the contrary, he is pointing consciously and directly to the earthly Jesus, and particularly to his servant life. That life, he proclaims, has a deeper-than-meets-the-eye reality: Jesus is uniquely of God, and so is that love which his words and actions so dramatically and powerfully made manifest. John's Logos Christ is the servant Christ of the earthly ministry.

It may, then, be more than fortuitous circumstance, and therefore an especially revealing commentary on the remarkable profundity of John's own Christian experience, that he alone of the four Evangelists tells of the time when Jesus performed the menial service of washing the feet of his disciples. They were puzzled that Jesus would, as they thought, so demean himself. Peter at first adamantly refused to accept either the love that was being offered or the demand that it made; but he capitulated because the power of Jesus' self-giving simply overwhelmed him. This is the way St. John tells the story:

> Jesus . . . rose from supper, laid aside his garments, and girded himself with a towel. Then he poured water into a basin, and began to wash the disciples' feet, and to wipe them with the towel with which he was girded. He came to Simon Peter; and Peter said to him, "Lord, do you wash my feet?" Jesus answered him, "What I am doing you do not know now, but afterward you will understand." Peter said to him, "You shall never wash my feet." Jesus answered him, "If I do not wash you, you have no part in me." Simon Peter said to him, "Lord, not my feet only but also my hands and my head!" . . . When he had washed their feet, and taken his garments, and resumed his place, he said to them, "Do you know what I have done to you? You call me Teacher and Lord; and you are right, for so I am. If I then, your Lord and Teacher, have washed your feet, you also ought to wash one another's feet. For I have given you an example, that you also should do as I have done to you. Truly, truly, I say to you, a servant is not greater than his master; nor is he who is sent greater than he who sent him. If you know these things, blessed are you if you do them" (Jn. 13:3–17).

This incident occurred, St. John intimates, in the famous upper room on the eve of Jesus' death. The time and circumstances were the same as those of the Last Supper. Many, noting that John alone of the Evangelists fails to describe Jesus' anticipatory giving of himself through the sharing of the bread and the cup, conclude that he has purposely substituted the footwashing in its place. In answer to the question, "Why?" it has been suggested that he was thereby seeking to lead his readers into a deeper understanding of the Eucharist's significance. Immediately, one recalls the problem at Corinth concerning the fellowship meals, which led St. Paul to speak so forcefully about *Agape*. It may well be that John's decision to substitute the incident of the footwashing was motivated by the same concern. That is, without neighbor love, the Eucharist is a travesty which brings only condemnation.

At least this is certain: No incident in the New Testament, short of the crucifixion itself, more vividly portrays the basic meaning of Jesus' life than does this picture of menial service. And the demand which it lays upon the Christian is that which lies at the heart of the New Morality: "You also ought to wash one another's feet." Ultimately, not law but love is God's way for his world.

V

Love and a Changing World

"Nothing matters but love." We have employed this slogan repeatedly because it cuts to the very heart of what the New Morality is all about, namely, that love is the sole inviolable "law," and hence the ultimate determiner for every thought, decision, word, action, and relationship. Admittedly, the slogan is something of a gimmick. These four words, for example, say nothing about what kind of love is meant. They hint nothing about how love is to be applied. They suggest nothing of the complexity and difficulty and hardship inherent in love's demand and love's task. Nevertheless, we have found that the New Testament picture of Christ-love in remarkably rich fashion supplies what is lacking. "Nothing matters but *Christian* love." To emend the statement in this way is to point to dimensions of meaning which have been neglected all too frequently in discussions of the New Morality.

More specifically, we have in these pages been asking a question. Adherents of the New Morality claim the authority of Jesus and of Holy Scripture for their position. Does the

evidence back up this claim? In our search for the answer we
have examined much of the New Testament in detail. And
each time that we have used the slogan, we have been forced
to take it more seriously. This is not, as we suggested at one
point, a matter subject to mechanical and definitive proof.
What we have found, however, is highly supportive of the
New Morality's claim.

Most important in this connection is the picture of Jesus
himself. He summarized man's entire existence under the
single word "love": love God, love neighbor. His teaching,
and even more his servant life of total self-giving to God and
man, make crystal clear love's priority and the nature of its
demand. Jesus was not an antinomian. Normally, he lived
within the framework of the laws of his community. But when
the law hindered rather than answered the genuine need of
persons, he did what love dictated. And he accepted the cross
and its total self-denial rather than betray what he held to be
God's own pattern for human existence.

St. Paul got the message. He knew that it was God's love
that had changed him and called him to a life of apostleship.
Not law, but faith which is demonstrably effective in neighbor-
love is all-important. Why the Apostle believed this so strongly
is clear. It was, of course, Christ with whom it all began and
in Christ that the Christian lives. And the Christ life was
(and is) the servant life. Quite simply, then, the Christian
must be as his Lord. Not always, we may feel, did Paul arrive
at correct decisions as to what servant love demands. One
might cite, for example, his seeming unawareness of the deeper
implications of slavery (1 Cor. 7:17–24). Nor can most people
today (and with good reason) wholeheartedly accept his essentially negative view of marriage (1 Cor. 7:1–9, 25–40). Our
questioning, however, should be gentle; we do not know all
the intricacies of the situations which he had to face. And,
most important, there is not the slightest doubt as to St. Paul's

ideal and intent. For him, faith and *Agape* are inseparable, and lack of love-in-action for others vitiates every good that man may cherish or endeavor.

St. John, too, knew Jesus as the servant Christ. Even more explicitly than St. Paul, he equates faith and right knowledge of the truth with the "doing" of *Agape*, and flatly asserts that love for God and indifference to others' needs are irreconcilable opposites. More than this, in Christ's self-sacrificing love John discerns the very inner being of God himself. And since God is love, and love is a "doing," man who is God's creature can find his own reason for being and become his true self only as he welcomes that love-in-action as the center of his life. As a result, we find in John's writings the most exclusive and strenuous underlining of love's imperative that there is in all of Holy Scripture.

According to the New Testament, then, that which lies at the heart of God's relationship with man, and of man's intended relationship with God and with his fellows, is love. Moreover, the same scriptural witness in many different ways testifies that Christian existence means staking one's life on love's pre-eminence. And the claim of the Christian New Morality, that the exclusive priority of love is both dominical and biblical, must be taken with the utmost seriousness.

Not only has *Agape*'s centrality for the New Testament ethic become clear, but we have also discovered much that helps us to determine what the nature of that love is. This is equally important because, as we indicated previously, misunderstanding on this point is probably the chief reason why many so lightly toss the New Morality aside as unworthy of serious consideration. More particularly, the misapprehension reveals itself in the charge that situationism's relativism (ultimately, whether or not an action is loving depends upon the situation) is but a thinly disguised rationalization for self-indulgence.

This, of course, depends upon what one means by "loving." And for the *Christian* ethic, the model is Christ-love. *Agape*, as we have seen at length, is completely antithetical to selfish permissiveness. In the New Testament, freedom from slavery to the law does not mean freedom from responsibility. On the contrary, it commits one to a new slavery to the servant Christ and hence to personal responsibility for every individual who has need. This plainly means that Christian love is unconditioned love. It makes no bargains such as, "If you love me, I'll love you." This is why *Agape* has its aegis not in one's emotions, nor in the attractiveness of its object, but in the will which is empowered by the Holy Spirit. One can readily recognize that there are those who, in the name of the New Morality, have equated situationism's flexibility with regard to pre-determined solutions with mere self-serving license. To some degree, at least, this may be attributable to the Situation Ethic's failure to establish adequately its root and its criteria in Holy Scripture. Much that passes for the New Morality in the popular view is long on freedom and short on that responsibility that dominated the life of Jesus of Nazareth. The result is actions which are thoroughly deserving of the sharp challenges which they evoke. A truly *Christian* New Morality, however, is as far removed from license and self-seeking as is day from night. The priority of Christ-love means the priority of one's neighbor.

As a specific example, one might cite problems of sexual behavior. Many, as we suggested earlier, find the freedom of the Situation Ethic especially alarming when they speculate about its application in this sensitive area of human concern. But here again, to understand the nature of biblical *Agape* is critically important. Actually, the Christian New Morality vigorously condemns every instance of sexual irresponsibility. Moreover, it cites Holy Scripture as its authority. But that authority, it should be noted, does not lie in the prohibitions attached to various kinds of sexual aberrations which are included in numerous New Testament lists of vices. These we can readily recognize as more or less adequate applications of the deeper underlying principle of *Agape*. In other words, the ultimate authority for responsibility in one's sexual conduct is precisely and simply the command "you shall love your neighbor." Sexual selfishness stands automatically proscribed as but one manifestation of that self-centeredness which biblical love condemns because, in whatever form, it manipulates persons as things existing solely for one's own advantage or pleasure. Adherents of the Christian New Morality, for instance, would be the first to insist that adultery in our contemporary society is a highly undesirable practice with consequences almost invariably destructive. But why? The answer is not because the prohibition of adultery is one of the Ten Commandments but, in the final analysis, because here is an act which, except in the most unusual circumstances, is harmful to persons. In other words, not law but love is the ultimate criterion—one which in this instance normally would confirm the traditional prohibition. And one may wonder whether that same criterion—*Agape*—does not perhaps offer a far greater long-range deterrent to every kind of sexual license than any formalized laws.

We must not, however, close our eyes to the other side of this coin. The very same principle—concern for the best good of persons—which so strongly indicts promiscuity demands that any Christian ethic raise sharp questions concerning traditional sexual mores. It is important to remember at this point that specifics about what *Agape* requires are integrally linked to the particular situation. And here it is imperative to realize that things have changed from what they were in the past. In recent years, our knowledge of what personhood is, and our awareness of the forces and factors which constitute it, have increased immeasurably. Particularly, we have gained new insight into the nature and function of human sexuality, and have recognized and welcomed more fully its pivotal role for an individual's wholeness. Inevitably, such new knowledge, conjoined with *Agape's* insistence upon the well-being of persons, gives rise to scrutiny of traditional patterns of sexual behavior. Any effective pastor, for example, whether he claims to be a situationist or not, knows that bad marriages can inhibit and warp personhood. He knows, too, that there are as many sexual indignities committed within the technical bond of marriage as without. Do our present attitudes and processes concerning divorce, birth control, and abortion actually reflect this awareness? Or, speaking more generally, are we so sure, after all, that in our very different world sex within marriage is always "loving" and that all other sex is invariably "unloving?" Such questions today are inevitable. And the New Morality's frequent concern with sexual matters, which has so often been misunderstood and used against it, is not a voyeuristic obsession, but a contemporary necessity. We now know that without candid acceptance of his sexuality, man cannot be himself. And if, as our analysis of the New Testament text strongly suggests, *Agape* does indeed take priority over all biblical sexual fiats, not to raise questions of this nature would be the height of irresponsibility.

The New Testament, then, proclaims the dignity of a freedom and a responsibility which are rooted in love. And whether in connection with man's sexuality or with any other area of human activity, to equate that freedom with license is totally erroneous. The Christian New Morality, because it is wholeheartedly committed to *Agape,* assumes more and demands more in terms of intelligence, self-discipline, and Christian commitment than is ever demanded of a legalism with ready-made answers. The New Morality's symbol is not the easy give and take of *Playboy* magazine, but the suffering servant of the cross.

Our examination of the New Testament has made plain the

biblical and theological roots of *Agape*. To understand this is to perceive that Christian situationism is not simply a momentary fad born of restlessness and adolescent rebellion, but an ethical perspective that is striving to determine what the servant Christ would say to the kind of world in which we find ourselves today. As time passes, the sensationalism which the New Morality currently provokes on the part of disputants and, regrettably, many adherents as well, will probably disappear. This will be all to the good. However, any ethic that truly has Christ-love as its center has an inherent permanency because, when all is said and done, its root is the age-old Christian gospel.

This fact, however, leads to another. The *Christian* New Morality has a relevance and a potential for good which many, including most Christian situationists themselves, have failed to spell out. In order to appreciate this, one must be fully aware of the character of our contemporary situation, and of its significance. As a summary description, the best single word is "change." And the old truisms that "life is change," that "time makes ancient good uncouth," and "that new occasions teach new duties," have been corroborated many times in recent years by extensive studies of cultural anthropology, and by the history of ethics in general. Nor can one exclude here the needs that man has or the values to which he subscribes. These also change. And an ethic that fails to take these realities of ongoing life seriously is bound to be rejected. "Status quoism" increasingly falls behind.

The relevance and the potential of the Christian New Morality stem from the fact that it does take change seriously and welcomes it. Its thoroughgoing commitment to *Agape* as the final arbiter in every situation makes two significant contributions to the contemporary scene. In the first place, the Christian New Morality refuses to worship as eternal verities the laws and customs of previous generations. These, it insists, have no inherent worth of their own. Their value, rather, for any age lies in the effectiveness with which they work for the good of persons—and even that good is bound to change as circumstances alter. Thus, freed from the past (although never rejecting prior experience as an important part of all decision-making), Christian situationism is realistically and refreshingly open to the future and, one might wish to add, providentially so; because there is nothing more distinctive in our time than new horizons, new complexities, and new possibilities for both good and evil beyond the wildest dreams of our forbears. In such a situation, openness and flexibility are qualities of critical importance. To be free from idolatry of the past is the first step toward readiness for the future.

The second contribution is equally noteworthy. The problems which the future promises are enormous. Solutions will not come easily, nor do Christian situationists have any illusion that they have or will have easy answers. However, the criterion of *Agape* is a specific and positive platform on which to stand. The Christian *knows*—that persons are more precious than all else and that, no matter what the circumstances and the complications are, the best good of persons is the end to be effected. And as an important corollary, and illustrating the permanency to which we referred, such an *Agape*-ethic is one that will continue to provide a significant key that can speak meaningfully to any and every culture in any and every kind of world that may develop in the future. For *Agape*, Christian situationism insists, *is* an eternal verity. And the preciousness of persons, and the right to the joy of full personhood—this, too, is the Christian gospel—are elements of the human situation which no circumstance can alter.

Again it may prove helpful to note specific current problems. Our purpose in each instance is not to provide solutions, but to suggest the kinds of questions that an *Agape*-ethic poses and the striking relevance that it has for all sorts of contemporary concerns.

One thinks, for example, of the population explosion. Its threat is incalculable. It is accelerating and deepening the dehumanization which is an inevitable consequence of under-privilege, starvation, and mass living conditions. Furthermore, it is rapidly despoiling the natural beauty which strengthens the human spirit. Even more critical, it is draining our natural resources and it is introducing an artificial imbalance that is already jeopardizing this planet's ecology. At stake is not only human survival, but as well human dignity and the possibility for individuals to live not as slaves to uncontrollable forces, but as full persons. Fortunately we have today the know-how adequate to defuse this population bomb. Although there are still those who idolize procreation as the one absolute of the married state, there has been a sweeping change of opinion on the matter of birth control during the past few generations. The obvious geometric progression of the world's population has forced us to re-think former convictions and decisions. And most would agree that Christian love demands a drastic intensifying of our efforts toward this end. It is noteworthy, too, that *Agape* has been the motivating criterion employed as a solution by countless people who have never heard of the Situation Ethic and who, as often as not, had no particular allegiance to formal Christianity. So it is, many would wish to add, that God the Holy Spirit works his will despite that idolizing of past tradition, which still characterizes a significant segment of Christian thinking.

To take another example, does not *Agape* raise particularly embarrassing questions about the current upswing of disorder in our cities? The unrest, of course, has many causes. Not least, however, it documents the progressively widening gap between the "haves" and the "have nots" that typifies not only our society, but the entire global community. Religious and political legalism may be tempted to castigate the "have nots" for their violence. Genuine love, however, will look more deeply. It will recognize that eruptions of violence are the inevitable result of an "unloving" situation. *Agape*, with its demand and power for good, has obvious and far-reaching implications in this context. Not the least of its contributions is the extremely uncomfortable challenge that it addresses to our total economic system that presently permits such disregard for persons. Is it not imperative that we seek and find a more "loving," and so more just, philosophy of economic relationship and distribution?

Closely related is the growing insistence of underprivileged peoples and new nations upon honest recognition of their needs and rights. Here, too, Christian concern for persons would seem to undercut our skillful rationalizations. Is not the grudging nature of our response to such obvious and legitimate need attributable to an idolizing of material things on the part of "the haves?" And yet, the Christian New Morality reminds us, the only "idol," the only absolute which man may "worship," is *Agape*. And *Agape* urges that the stirrings of the "have nots" are no mere prideful longing for a place in the sun, but a just cry to be allowed that fullness of living which the Christian gospel affirms to be the right of every human being. In all the voluminous pages of the Bible, both the Old Testament and the New Testament, there is not one single word that can be legitimately interpreted as justifying or condoning, much less authorizing or demanding, that servile status to which our society still massively condemns others of God's children. One thing, however, Holy Scripture does demand—the risk of self-denying love.

Wherever we look today, the potential and the applicability of the Christian New Morality's fundamental criterion are evident. For example, what does the well-being of persons say to the selfish interests that are permitting air pollution to bring our cities perilously close to mass suicide? Should not *Agape* make us uneasy when we contemplate a system of lobbying that absolutizes the self-interest of power blocs to the detriment of the greatest number? Or what of the vexing problem of civil disobedience in the light of the legitimate need for, and best interest of, community. Over and beyond current situations, however, are others that we can see on the horizon. These even more dramatically illustrate the need for an alternative to pat generalities that are supplied by the past. We are on the threshold of selective human breeding through the use of genetics. The indefinite prolongation of life through transplants and suspended animation, and intelligence stimulation and thought control, are imminent probabilities. We may well discover other forms of life in the solar system. More and more, as time passes, we shall uncover the basic secrets of life itself. Every one of these impending situations can be turned to man's great good. However, all will pose staggering problems.

In every example which we have cited, it is personhood, and the opportunity to live meaningful, creative, and rewarding lives that are at stake. And the complexities of today's world make impossible the luxury and the illusory security of the simple fiats of a biblical or ecclesiastical legalism. The high potential of the Christian New Morality derives from its single-minded insistence that every attempt at decision-making must commence with the question, "What will best enable an individual to be that full person which, by divine right, he can be?" The priority of *Agape* over every other consideration offers precisely that flexibility with regard to the past and openness toward the future that is demanded by the exciting and puzzling newness of the contemporary scene. More than this, the Christian New Morality speaks with authority and with urgency, because its criterion of servant love is grounded in the biblical and theological understanding of God as revealed in Christ, and so is intrinsic to the Christian faith.

Among Christians these days there is much talk not only of a new ethic, but also of new theology, new liturgy, and of new experimental forms of ministry. This hopeful ferment

and upspringing of life within the church has as its exterior
cause those same contemporary realities that are forcing re-
appraisal of the traditions and the norms of the past in every
area of human concern. And again, the sharp relevance of the
Situation Ethic is apparent because of what it is saying to
institutional Christianity: The world is changing at breakneck
speed, new circumstances demand the humility of self-exami-
nation, and, above all, the church must re-discover her role
as the servant of the world.

Servanthood is inherent in the very nature of the church
because she is Christ's, and her life is the life in Christ. As
Jesus was sent, so is the church sent. As he was a servant, so
is she. The good news that love is of God, and is an effective
power which makes all things whole and new, will be laughed
out of court wherever and whenever the church, whose gospel
this is, fails to witness to its truth in her own daily life.

For that matter, the laughter can be heard today. Criticism
of institutional Christianity is as strong within the church as
without. Her power, it is said, is much more that of big business and bureaucracy rather than the enabling of the Holy
Spirit. This charge is hard to deny when one realizes how
much of her material support comes from investments which
condone the suppression of millions. The church, it is claimed,
is far more concerned with a jealous guardianship of the status
quo—tradition, orthodoxy of thought, "the plant," possessions
—than with the risk of mission. And again one thinks of her
retreat from the inner city to the pseudo-respectability of the
suburbs, of her defensive suspicion of frontier thinking, or of
diversionary concern with liturgical preciousness at the ex-
pense of the cries of the hungry. Are new altars and new
organs really more important than bread and decent housing
and sound education? Too frequently, it is charged, the
church tacitly encourages her members to use her as a haven
from the world, and preaches a "pie-in-the-sky" gospel of selfish personal salvation which neither recognizes nor cares what

the real "down-to-earth" needs and concerns of people are. Has
she forgotten St. John's warning that fullnes of life cannot be
attained in isolation from one's fellows? And what of the
New Testament witness that love for God and neighbor are
one seamless robe?

It is true that there is growing awareness of these imbalances
and deficiencies. There are stirrings and increasing attempts,
here and there, to rearrange priorities. Still, however, within
the church as a whole there is neither massive concern nor
massive commitment to the servant life. As a result, the material and ideational gap between those who have and those
who have not widens every day, as does the gap between
the church and the real world; and the cry goes out: "Where
is the church in our time?" One of my students recently expressed his alarm with these words: "The church can become
so absorbed with religious technicalities that she tends to
withdraw herself from the world outside. The people of these
churches may indeed love God, but it will be a God that is too
small. They may indeed love their neighbors, but their neighbors will be too few. The narrowness of this kind of religion
and the minutiae of its technicalities may become so absorb-
ing as actually to prevent the worshipper from seeing the real
purpose any church must have in order to be a useful element
and instrument for God's work in his world. This is the demand for the church to reach out into the world, and to love
the people in the world, for Christ's sake, where and as they
are."

To today's church in today's situation the Christian New
Morality speaks a loud warning. It challenges her to re-discover her reason for being. Its insistence that "nothing matters
but love" is a demand for the church's renewal, a demand
which is backed by dominical and biblical authority, and a
renewal which is far more deep-rooted than most have had the
courage to imagine. *Agape* insists that people are more sacred
than buildings and liturgies, and that theological orthodoxy

is right theology, true to the gospel, and deserving of a hearing, only if it effectively communicates the priority and the urgency of love's "doing." It reminds us that the Christ, whose body the church is, was and remains the servant Christ, and that the church's role is to witness, not only through her own inner life but equally through her thrust out into the world, to the hardship *and* the joy of Christ-love. It challenges her exaggerated concern with the past and with future rewards by underlining the much neglected truth that the gospel speaks to man's immediate *now*, and by recalling that love is a creative and redemptive power that recognizes and responds to and can supply every human need. The Christian New Morality begs for a return to the Christ who is the incarnation of love, God's own love-in-action, and therefore invites the joyful re-discovery that wherever love is or is needed, there is Christ, as much out in the world and waiting to be found as he is in the churches, where today his true nature is often unrecognized. In short, the church is called as was her Teacher and Lord to wash the feet of the world; and if she and her members cannot see that God is present and active and waiting to be recognized and welcomed in the everyday affairs of men, then both she and her people should regard all that they are and do with deep suspicion.

Organized Christianity today is restless, baffled at the speed with which the world is passing it by, and frustrated by the new intricacies of late twentieth century existence. And yet, the Christian New Morality confidently declares, the good news of servant love and of its irresistible power is precisely what the world awaits. The church must surrender her concern for self in order that in Christ she may be reborn as prophetic judge, lover, and healer of all mankind: "Awake, O sleeper, and arise from the dead, and Christ shall give you light" (Eph. 5:14).

When former values and patterns of thinking and behavior

are being challenged as severely as is the case today, there is bound to be a feeling of personal "lostness," and a revival of age-old questioning of the most fundamental kind: "Who am I? Why am I? How am I?" The increased use of narcotics, the rise in alcoholism, the disintegration of society on many fronts, and a pervading sense of alienation all testify to the magnitude of man's present personal insecurity. For many, the pace of change is too rapid and the problems too enormous. What, if any, is the reason for being?

Even to this deepest of concerns the Christian New Morality speaks clearly. And its special insight is this—that man's questions about his "being" cannot be answered apart from questions directed toward his actions. "What shall I do? How shall I conduct myself? What is my proper interaction with the world and with other people?"—in these queries, since love-in-action is God's own way with the world, lies the clue to meaning. And to contemporary man's "lostness" the message is this: Always there is a purpose for one's existence; that purpose is to act, that is, to give of one's self to others.

The Christian New Morality, then, answers man's search for meaning with the "doing" of the gospel. Hence, it offers the gift of personal identity, because to have a task to perform is the key to dignity and self-respect, and is essential for personal fulfillment. Furthermore, here is a calling that everyone in his own way can embrace and fulfill; because those who lack special talents or abilities are no less able to give of themselves for others' benefit than can those who are peculiarly gifted. More than this, the "doing" of servant love is a vocation which the Christian knows to be worthwhile, creative, and always a right beginning—even when, as so often today, it is difficult to decide where we should go from here. St. John, especially, has made this clear. Love is of God, and in loving action for others one is living in harmony with the very warp and woof of God's universe.

Man's search for meaning is, of course, integrally related to his search for God. Here again St. John's particular understanding of the Situation Ethic's criterion, Christ-love, offers an encouragement. There are, some may wish to argue, various ways in which man can apprehend God. However, there is one way, John would say, of which we may always be sure—and that is to be "up and doing" in the pattern of the servant love of Christ. In other words, the Christian New Morality affirms, "Where love is enacted, there God is." And to him who is struggling to find the clue to his own existence, the Christian New Morality says, "Love. Act. God is not remote. God is not dead. God is not a vague future hope. *God Is Now.*"

Clearly, the Christian New Morality necessitates boldness and a deep faith. It occasions no surprise, however, that many people, even Christians, are fearful in times of rapid change, and cling with special fervor to the status quo and to the seeming security of a more tranquil past. For such individuals, of course, the Situation Ethic poses a threat. To this circumstance also St. John speaks. It's almost as if he actually envisaged the kind of world in which we presently live. He records this saying of Jesus which counsels optimism and courage to the timid and the fearful: "The Holy Spirit, whom the Father will send in my name, he will teach you all things, and bring to your remembrance all that I have said to you" (Jn. 14:26).

"The Holy Spirit . . . will teach you all things," or, as the thought is expressed elsewhere, "When the Spirit of truth comes, he will guide you into all the truth" (Jn. 16:13). St. John, like St. Paul, knows the Spirit as enabling power. Even more, however, he stresses the Spirit's role as a teacher and revealer who in each successive generation will guide believers into a richer experience of human existence and into a right understanding of Christ's way and Christ's will in every conceivable situation. We can well imagine, then, that with such deep faith in the Holy Spirit, John would not shy away from our kind of world. Instead, he would embrace its changeableness and confusion as the "stirring-up" of the God who is ever now.

John, that is, would be the first to say that to absolutize the past is to limit man's vision and creativity, and to close his heart. In the challenges of today he would hear the Holy Spirit saying, "Thus far you have come; well and good. But now is God's time to move ahead!" His view of every new problem would be a positive one. Our culture's preoccupation with sex, for instance, even when it expresses itself in ways that on all counts seem totally perverse, would not repel him. Here, rather, he would see a yearning which is good, one based upon the correct intimation that sexual love is a God-given gift that is essential to life's wholeness. And he would plead that Christian concern create a sexual morality that makes full realization of this treasure possible. Nor would St. John look upon the restlessness of today's young people as mere selfish permissiveness rebelling against authority. Instead, he would point to youth's awareness, however inchoate, that there is a meaning, a richness, and a beauty to living which escapes them. And he would point out, perhaps not too gently, that at least partly to blame are the idolizing of tradition and custom, and the legalism of a status quo perspective, all of which are fostered to no small extent by those two pillars of our culture, the church and the university, and all of which inhibit the free flow of creative seeking which is in every man. And in the oncoming economic dislocation which automation is causing, St. John would see the possibility for man, as never before, to gain in stature and in rewarding creativity—*if* *Agape* is allowed to have its way. No, St. John would not be afraid. All of this, he would say, is the wonderful work of the Spirit who seeks to blast us out of our fear and need for security, to recall us to the insecurity of a self-giving suffering church, and to win us over to that daring boldness and power

of love which is of God himself. The openness of Christ-
love is openness to the Spirit which can and will "teach you
all things."

In another way, too, St. John encourages those who are
afraid for the future. For equally significant in John 14:26 is
the assurance that the same Spirit who seeks to move us boldly
into the future will also "bring to your remembrance all that
I have said to you." In other words, one need not fear that the
many new possibilities that lie ahead and that must be, will
rob us of those great goods and treasures of the past that are of
lasting consequence.

Always, that is, the new will find its truest and fullest meaning in that which was once and for all given: the Christ. As
the centuries pass, increasingly "you will know the truth, and
the truth will make you free"—but again, what is meant here
is the truth about Jesus Christ (Jn. 8:32). If, that is, the times
demand a new theology, the new must be a more meaningful
and winning expression of man's encounter with the same
Christ. Any new liturgy must proclaim with greater clarity
the same mighty acts of God as these have been summed up in
Christ. New forms of ministry must have as their only purpose
the more effective mediating of the servanthood of Christ.
And so it must be for those new circumstances, new insights,
new solutions, and new methods with which the New Morality
is so concerned—they must be examined and devised and as-
similated and applied with the love of Christ. And ultimately,
any morality which is Christian will bring to every moment of
decision-making the same Christ of the New Testament, he
who ever lives as the one through whom God's "nowness" is
revealed as self-giving love.

Bibliography

The following books and articles have been chosen to represent a broad spectrum of opinion, including perceptive criticism, with respect to Situation Ethics. Those singled out by an asterisk offer the best introduction to the New Morality:

Cox, Harvey, ed., *The Situation Ethics Debate*. Philadelphia: Westminster Press, 1968.

Dodd, C. H., *Gospel and Law: The Relation of Faith and Ethics in Early Christianity*. New York: Columbia University Press, 1951 (4th printing, 1957).

Fletcher, Joseph, *Moral Responsibility: Situation Ethics at Work*. Philadelphia: Westminster Press, 1967.

*Fletcher, Joseph, *Situation Ethics: The New Morality*. Philadelphia: Westminster Press, 1966.

Knox, John, *The Ethics of Jesus in the Teaching of the Church: Its Authority and Relevance*. New York: Abingdon Press, 1961.

Lehmann, Paul, *Ethics in a Christian Context*. New York: Harper and Row, 1963.

Oden, Thomas C., *Radical Obedience: The Ethics of Rudolf Bultmann*. Philadelphia: Westminster Press, 1964.

Outka, Gene H. and Ramsey, Paul, eds., *Norm and Context in Christian Ethics*. New York: Charles Scribner's Sons, 1968.

Pike, James A., *You & the New Morality—74 Cases*. New York: Harper and Row, 1967.

Pittenger, W. Norman, *Love is the Clue*. London: A. R. Mowbray, 1967.

Ramsey, Paul, *Basic Christian Ethics*. New York: Charles Scribner's Sons, 1950.

Ramsey, Paul, *Deeds and Rules in Christian Ethics*. New York: Charles Scribner's Sons, 1967.

Rhymes, Douglas, *No New Morality: Christian Personal Values and Sexual Morality*. London: Constable, 1964.

*Robinson, John A. T., *Christian Morals Today*. Philadelphia: Westminster Press, 1964.

"The New Morality—What, Why—and Why Not?" A symposium in *Religion in Life*, Vol. 35, No. 2, pp. 170-229.

Williams, Harry A., "Theology and Self-Awareness," in A. R. Vidler, ed., *Soundings: Essays Concerning Christian Understanding*. Cambridge: Cambridge University Press, 1966.